GW00715919

GRAND PRIX '88

GRAND PRIX '88

**ROGER MOODY &
STUART SYKES**

BBC BOOKS

ABOUT THE AUTHORS

Roger Moody had his first taste of motor-racing when his father took him as a boy to a hill climb at Shelsley Walsh near the family home in the Midlands. Later Hednesford Hills circuit became a favourite place to visit before a career in journalism, radio and television took over.

When BBC Television Sport recommenced its coverage of Formula One racing in 1978 Roger was part of the production team, eventually becoming producer of the *Grand Prix* programme. Today he is a member of Television Sport's management team with special responsibilities for contracts – but maintains a keen interest in motor-racing and journalism. He is married with two children and lives in Surrey.

For Stuart Sykes, motor-racing has been a passion since boyhood days in the Scottish Borders were filled with the name of rising star Jim Clark, and Ecurie Ecosse were performing heroic feats at Le Mans.

Despite a long detour via University teaching, one advantage of which was a year's stay in Le Mans itself, Stuart saw the light and worked for four years on the BBC's Ceefax sports desk before moving into motor sport full time. Spells with Ken Tyrrell and Ecurie Ecosse themselves have been part and parcel of his time in motor-racing public relations and as a freelance journalist.

Published by BBC Books
a division of BBC Enterprises Limited,
Woodlands, 80 Wood Lane, London W12 0TT

First published 1988
© Roger Moody and Stuart Sykes 1988

ISBN 0 563 20648 9

Typeset by Ace Filmsetting Ltd, Frome, Somerset
Printed and bound in England by Redwood Burn Ltd,
Trowbridge, Wiltshire
Colour separation by Technik
Cover printed by Fletchers

Photograph on page 2: *One face of Formula 1: fire marshal at Monaco*

CONTENTS

A new driving force for '88: a McLaren–Honda with possible future World Champion Ayrton Senna in the cockpit

FOREWORD BY AYRTON SENNA

I suppose I'm almost as British as I am Brazilian! I won the British Formula Ford Championships in 1981 and 1982 and the British Formula Three title in 1983. My first Formula One drive was for Ted Toleman in 1984 and for the last three years I've been trying very hard to win the drivers' title for that ever-so-British team that Colin Chapman founded – Lotus. I even once lived at Esher in Surrey – and you can't get more British than that! I love the people in the United Kingdom, their humour and their race-tracks – but I don't like the weather in Great Britain!

Since my racing brought me to England BBC Television Sport has followed my career and I hope you have all enjoyed watching me on *Sunday Grandstand* or on *Grand Prix* as much as I have enjoyed racing all round the world.

Now I'm really going for that elusive World Drivers' Championship at McLaren. I really believe 1988 is going to be good, presenting a new challenge for me – a new team, an engine I got to know at Lotus, and the best possible team-mate in twice World Champion Alain Prost alongside me.

Like Alain said when he wrote a foreword to the first *BBC Grand Prix* book – 'thanks for your support'. I hope for all my British fans both the drivers' and the teams' championships come back to Woking again.

Top *Engineering in style: Ken Tyrrell (standing), Maurice Phillippe and Data General CAD system*

Bottom *Oily rag days: Silverstone 1948*

1 ENGINEERS AND OILY RAGS

A Grand Prix (GP) team is a curious animal indeed. Existing solely to create highly-specialised machines for men to race in, it is a complex piece of machinery in itself, a whole whose function must be greater than the sum of its parts. After all, it puts human lives on the line once a fortnight on average from March until November, to say nothing of the countless hours of testing that are the modern GP driver's lot. And as the parts in question differ as widely as do those in any human gathering, so the lubricant employed to ease friction, cool temperatures and tempers and make all run smoothly is simple to define but hard to find: an endless supply of patience and perseverance allied to unfailing determination to be the best. Additives such as tact and good humour will help, of course, but what keeps this particular engine stoked is raw human energy.

At least, that used to be the case: in the early days of GP racing a wing and a prayer were as likely to get you to the end of the race as are today's aerodynamic devices, and driving by the seat of the pants was the norm rather than driving by numbers or computer program. GP racing has come a long way, however, since the World Championship got off the ground in 1950. Only five teams contested that first season of seven races, one of which in any case was at Indianapolis in the United States and did not attract the European contingent. It says much for Ferrari, in fact, that the Italian marque was in at the beginning of GP racing as we now know it, and that two victories in a row to finish the 1987 season signalled the continuing strength of the Maranello regime.

By 1958, when the Constructors' World Championship was introduced in parallel with the Drivers' competition, the ranks had swollen to six, three of them British: Vanwall, BRM and Lotus, though a year later the numbers were down to four. Only in the mid-sixties did the list of manufacturers wishing to win the sport's highest honour begin to approach double figures, and we had to wait until 1973 to see that particular landmark reached. Since then the figure has gone as high as seventeen, in 1981 and 1982, while 1987 saw sixteen teams take part in World Cham-

Top *Winning combination: Jonathan Palmer in the 1987 Tyrrell at Loews Hairpin, Monaco*

Bottom *Silverstone 1985: Frank Williams in charge*

pionship races, and the new season seemed likely to better that figure as new Formula One concerns sprang up in the strangest places.

It is a matter for some national pride, therefore, that the teams which carried off the 1987 Constructors' World Championships – one for turbo-charged, the other (unkindly labelled 'Second Division') for normally-aspirated cars – were both British. Williams Grand Prix Engineering and the Tyrrell Racing Organisation have become national institutions in their own right, but both concerns knew oily-rag days of their own before making it to the top of the GP tree. If the Tyrrells, by dint of success in the Colin Chapman Trophy, were somewhere in the middle of the Formula One hierarchy overall in 1987, they plan in 1988 to be back where Williams undoubtedly are for the time being: in number one spot.

Before looking at some of the people and practicalities that shape the GP world today, let us look more closely at the team of the eighties. But as a counterweight, we will look just as closely at a team which made a welcome return to Formula One last season and whose plans for 1988 are proof of their own ambition. More of them later . . .

Team of the eighties? McLaren and, to a lesser extent, Ferrari may dispute that title, but Williams Grand Prix Engineering began the decade with two successive Constructors' World Championships, have just done the double again, and for good measure have given three drivers – Alan Jones, Keke Rosberg and Nelson Piquet -- the wherewithal to acquire titles of their own. In many ways, Williams are a microcosm of the modern GP world. The company has expanded beyond most people's wildest expectations since Frank Williams entered the sport in the seventies as a team manager, and while it now demonstrates all that is best and most successful in motor-racing, undeniably the pressures are there for all to see.

With four GP wins in 1985, nine in 1986 and nine again in 1987, Williams would appear to be at their peak. But for accident, injury and mechanical failures in the final two races of last season, in fact, they would have established a new record total for points accumulated in the World Championship. Three times they have broken the magical 100-point barrier in the process of breaking McLaren's mid-eighties stranglehold on the spoils of Formula One. But it was not always so . . . Coming into motor-racing as a budding driver in the sixties, Frank Williams – like Ken Tyrrell – quickly realised his talents lay in managing the driving skills of others and turned to running his own team. Called by other names at first in deference to sponsors, Williams was born out of a crisis in 1976 when the Wolf was literally at the door. Canadian magnate Walter Wolf had seemed about to solve all the team's sponsorship problems when he suddenly broke the partnership and took all the assets with him.

Right *Different team kit, same men in charge: Frank Williams and Patrick Head*

Below *Different clothes for the car, too: the Williams in Leyland sponsorship guise*

Necessity, however, is the mother of invention, and in true oily-rag fashion Frank Williams wiped his hands, rolled up his sleeves and resolved to get his own – his very own – enterprise off the ground. Recruitment of such talented men as Chief Designer Patrick Head did nothing to hinder the cause, with the result that by 1979 Williams cars were winning GPs – Clay Regazzoni's victory at Silverstone that year was the first – and a year later lifting crowns. A Queen's Award for Export Achievement (unique in Formula One) ensued in 1981, and at Christmas 1983 Frank gave himself a substantial present by moving lock, stock and barrel into the splendid, purpose-built Grand Prix Engineering facility described in our first *BBC Grand Prix* book.

If Head's first designs, and especially the FW07, were the stuff of racing legend, the same was to be true of the cars he planned around the new power units Williams acquired from Honda, in a partnership struck up that same year. That alliance is now at an end, as is related elsewhere, but for three years in particular, 1985 through 1987, the combination was the winningest in Formula One. As one of the design staff at Williams' Didcot facility, who used to work for the Ministry of Defence, was heard to say: 'I used to be involved with free-flight rockets – we just put wheels on them now!'

The keys to this phenomenal success, in Frank Williams' own words, are the harnessing of human skills and energies to a single purpose and the creation of a framework in which teamwork is all. 'Every one of these people is worth his weight in gold,' he enthuses as he talks of the hundred-strong workforce around him, while the term 'genius' is the one he applies to Head himself. But to assist this human machine Williams also employ the most up-to-date technology in their pursuit of victories. 'This is all about winning races' is another of Frank's favourite expressions, and to that aim Williams use the General Electric CALMA CAD/CAM system to accelerate and refine their analysis and production.

We all may be familiar with the occasional cad in motor sport, but CAD may be a new term to some. It stands for Computer Aided Design, while CAM is the next stage, Computer Aided Manufacture, and it is a system used – to varying degrees, as we shall see – by a number of the teams in today's GP world. Oily rags? Not now – you need soft cloths to clean the screens on sophisticated engineering work-stations which are taking design offices into the twentieth century and the one beyond. The beauty of such systems lies in doing what GP drivers always want to do: save time. With access to mainframe computers capable of processing six million instructions per second, CAD/CAM software can pare hours and even days off processes that in oily-rag days cost many men as many late nights.

Take, for example, a suspension system. First of all, its parts have to be strong and rigid, but light – the saving of weight is also paramount; but then, as components in a complex structure reacting to the enormous loadings placed on a speeding GP car, each of these parts has a knock-on effect on the ones arranged around it, so any modification to one will require concomitant alteration of the whole. In the good old days this would have meant endless patience in the redrawing of all such parts, whereas today's systems are able to project three-dimensional models on to a screen, accept modification, and incorporate it into the design and production of the next-generation suspension of any given car.

Stress analysis, systems analysis, the logging of performance parameters and their subsequent interpretation for future use: the applications of the CAD concept are far-reaching, and though costly they are the norm for the forward-looking GP team. The control they give over all aspects of a car's production is matched by their ability to interface with sophisticated electronic information-retrieval systems that will allow the team in question to communicate with other users all over the world – and in a sport as international as Formula One that is a major advantage.

To that must be added the sheer peace of mind afforded Frank Williams by the manufacturing of so many of his cars' components in the Williams plant itself. From the carbon fibre and other composites for the chassis to the suspension and gearbox parts, so much emanates directly from the Didcot factory that quality control is no longer a nightmare – a point to which our other team manager in the spotlight will return. With a full-scale in-house public relations department to set alongside the Research and Development team headed up by Frank Dernie, the accountancy section and workshop staff, Williams is in many ways the model of the GP team of today; and with other projects such as tyre work for the Ministry of Defence originating in its R and D department, the company has pointed the way towards diversification in the never-ending search for balance between pushing back the frontiers of automotive knowledge and the basic task of winning races.

On the all-important sponsorship front, too, Williams have led the way, and in a sense they are unique in not having settled for one major sponsor who literally buys all the space on the car. Hence the multi-coloured appearance of the Williams in the eighties, for after early tie-ups with Saudia Airlines that gave the car rather less crowded livery, Williams now boast Canon, Mobil, ICI, Denim and Barclay – companies, that is, from oil to aftershave, from cameras to composite materials for the space age. What is the rationale behind these multiple tie-ins? Frank Williams gives the straightforward answer: 'Our philosophy has always been to endeavour to be associated with substantial companies who not only have

Left *Ken Tyrrell: happy with DG tie-in*

Above *CAD in action: DG screen with car model*

obvious financial resources but also very important technical resources too. With that sort of backing it means that our "little" high-technology company is associated with large corporations and we complement each other.'

This reasoning, incidentally, echoes the words of Ken Tyrrell when he discusses the link-up with the Data General Corporation that not only saved the financial day for Tyrrell at the start of 1986, but also gave him an in-house CAD/CAM system that is now the envy of the GP world and has helped Ken to a World Championship in the normally-aspirated division as well as taking his driver Jonathan Palmer to a World Championship of his own. A 'strategic alliance' was how Data General chose to describe their arrangement with Tyrrell. If the term 'sponsorship' implies that someone comes and throws a bucket of money at a racing team, a strategic alliance is intended to show that this is very much a two-way process. A sponsor from the right walk of life – high-tech, high profile – can use the Formula One car not just as a very mobile form of advertising, but also as a high-speed test-bed for its own equipment. Few proving-grounds can be as competitive as this one, after all.

As we saw with Williams, however, it is not only the computer or indus-try-related giants who can profit from exposure on a GP car. The purpose of the tobacco companies is obvious – to achieve worldwide windows on their goods as other marketing strategies are gradually closed to them by government edict or patterns of social behaviour. Be that as it may, 'fag-packet cars' are still very much part and parcel of the GP scene and will be for the foreseeable future. In the case of Williams, this aspect is less

But there are still other tools of the trade . . .

obvious than with some 'wholly-owned' cars, and one of the names on the Williams machines, Denim, is not there because of the oily-rag image.

'Grand Prix racing', said a spokesman at the start of Denim's involvement with Williams in 1983, 'is a sport demanding exceptional levels of self-confidence, skill and courage. It fits perfectly into our image of the Denim Man [their capitals], who is a competitor and a winner who enjoys, and deserves, a sophisticated, exciting and international life style.' Well . . . scepticism about marketing hype apart, the association must have been fruitful, for the company is still there on the car today, and like most sponsors sends its own public relations person to the GPs themselves to gain maximum exposure from the drivers' deeds of derring-do. To see the exploitation of media coverage, the marketing of ancillaries such as leisure wear, the use of GPs as occasions for VIP entertaining, is to watch another well-oiled machine in action that has little to do with the days of oily rags but engineers maximum benefit from the world's most visible sport.

All of these people, whether directly connected with the Williams team or not, are involved in the teamwork which is one of the themes of this book as it investigates the workings of Formula One. For some observers, though, cracks showed in the Williams team in 1987 and did some damage to the image those very sponsors are so anxious to be reflected in. The worst were the splits so evident between drivers Nigel Mansell and Nelson Piquet, the latter taking the world title despite winning three

Good-humoured plea from Nigel!

races to Mansell's six, a feat the Englishman backed up with eight pole positions and an unprecedented run of fifteen successive starts from the front row. A failure to communicate those little improvements which mean so much to a car's performance, but might also help make your team-mate faster . . . public utterances which ranged from the wryly disparaging to the openly hostile . . . public displays of temper, on more than one occasion, indeed: this is the stuff of internecine warfare, not the mix required to keep a GP engine-room running at optimum output, surely? Frank Williams will have none of this. 'Their rivalry was grossly over-exaggerated by the press,' he retorts, 'and of very scant interest to me. What *is* of interest to me is that in 1987 we won far more races than anyone else and won both World Championships by a very long way indeed.' Fair comment, and just what you would expect from a man who has recovered from near-fatal injury in a car accident to lead his team from a wheelchair in the pit lane of the GP circuits of the world.

Nevertheless, the adverse criticism levelled at the Williams camp on more than one occasion in 1987 is perhaps a sign of the times in that the company's very size and success, in this most exposed terrain, has laid it open to often-withering crossfire from that most fickle of friends, the press. With Piquet departed in search of Honda engines in 1988 – more of this later, too – and Riccardo Patrese now lining up with Mansell in the Williams cockpits, there may be rather less tension at the top, and the team may be allowed to get on with the business in hand, namely winning

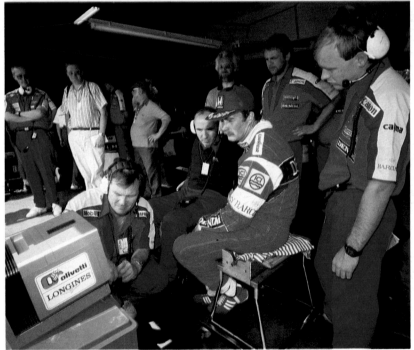

Top *Team-mates need to beat each other first: Piquet heads Mansell in Mexico 1987, but Nigel won his sixth – and last – of the year*

Bottom *Back fully in command: Frank in the Williams pit*

yet more races. The reversion to normally-aspirated engines for the forth-coming campaign will have no effect, says Frank, on the budgets, which will continue to grow as they have over the last decade, so the need to maintain good relations with those sponsors is perhaps greater than ever.

Teamwork, however, is all: and in 1987 Williams gave nine winning examples of that teamwork in action. Perhaps the finest, though, came at a race where they did not win. In Portugal we had one of those first-lap pile-ups that were all too frequent in 1987 – more of this, too, anon – but which gave the teams the chance to show what they could do under real pressure. Nelson Piquet's car had gone off on the first corner in a com-ing-together with Michele Alboreto's Ferrari, and limped home with more than a little damage to its undertray. As the grid re-formed for the second start and work on the cars was allowed, Chief Mechanic Alan Challis – one of the most experienced on the GP scene – led the Williams pit crew into action on Piquet's car, and with a remarkable demonstration of co-ordinated expertise they had it ready for the off and spared the Brazilian the annoyance of having to switch to his reserve machine. It was, per-haps, a small incident, but the manner – and particularly the spirit – of its accomplishment were a joy to behold.

Before leaving the top of the tree for what might rather unfairly be called the bottom, for reasons that should emerge, there is time for a pit stop of our own, to greet a driver rather than a team manager, and one whose popularity in this country and elsewhere has happily not dimin-ished as his GP fortunes have waned. Derek Warwick is possibly the most likeable man to wear a GP crash hat, and one of the most refresh-ingly accessible. Getting close now to the 100 GPs mark, the Hampshire man made the most promising start to his Formula One career with Toleman, suffered outrageous fortune with the Renault demise in 1985, and after a fruitless year with a disastrous Brabham car in 1986 took a meagre three points from the 1987 campaign at the wheel of one of the Arrows cars. The famous Warwick optimism is undented, however, and the question is whether Arrows can bridge the gap from lower-middle order to top-flight team in time for Derek to enjoy some of his just rewards.

'We have a great saying at Arrows at the moment,' comes the reply. ' "It's going to be great in '88!" And I can honestly say that I've never felt more optimistic at the start of a season. After our last two test runs I feel as good as I have done any year since I came into Formula One.' The basic cause of this outburst of enthusiasm is one that has characterised GP racing – dogged, some would say – for several years, notably since the introduction of turbocharged engines with their sharply-varying

Left *Youthful Derek Warwick as family businessman*

Below *Disappointing times: Derek in the Renault*

Bottom *And it wasn't all easy with Arrows in 1987 . .*

power outputs and questionable reliability. 'We've made a real break-through on the engine front,' opines Warwick. 'We have top men from both BMW and Renault joining Heini Mader [the Swiss specialist respon-sible for the Arrows team's Megatron engine preparation], and I think we shan't lose our way there again as we did a little in the middle of last season. Added to which, running at 2.5 bar of turbo boost in line with the new regulations seems to suit us very well.'

Not for Arrows the frantic rush to build an all-new car in time for the first major testing, at Rio in March, as Warwick and his team-mate Eddie Cheever were happy with the performance of the A10 in 1987. 'Yes, we're keeping the same car, which Eddie and I both got on so well with at the start of last year; and we enjoy increased support from an excellent sponsor in USF&G, so I believe it is possible for Arrows to move up from being a midfield team to one of the front-runners.' Does this mean an upturn at last, then, in the Warwick career? 'Well, it's got to, hasn't it?' is the honest answer. 'I'm not getting any younger [Derek is 34 in 1988] but I am fitter than I've ever been, and ready for one last effort to re-establish myself. Arrows could be the springboard, for it's very much an up-and-coming team, and I still feel I can win championships.' Derek had just fin-ished a game of squash when he made those remarks. How did he feel after the match? 'Oh, you always feel great when you're winning, don't you?' Many are those who would like to see Warwick do a Mansell and get on the winner's rostrum at last.

And so to the bottom of the tree. This is meant with not the slightest dis-respect to the team involved, but said only because they finished at the bottom of the World Championship standings in that 'Second Division' normally-aspirated class of which we spoke earlier. Despite that appar-ently dismal statistic, March Engineering is one of the most famous and successful names in motor-racing, and the truth of the matter is that 1987 saw the return of March to Formula One for the first time in many years during which they concentrated on building cars for others to race in different categories of motor sport.

In Formula One since the South African Grand Prix of 1970, March can boast of three World Championship race wins. Jackie Stewart took the chequered flag in Spain in 1970 for Ken Tyrrell in a March while the Sur-rey team manager was waiting for his own first car to be completed; the solitary win for Vittorio Brambilla came in a March in Austria in 1975; and a year later the great Ronnie Peterson was victorious in a March in Italy, though his was the last great name to be associated with the marque. Third in the Constructors' Championship in 1970 and 1971, March scored no points at all after 1976.

This did not signal a decline but rather a change of direction. Founded

in 1969, March Engineering has developed its own special formula for making cars in which people win races in every category of motor sport, earning a CBE for Robin Herd, the genius behind it all, and seeing well over 1000 cars roll off the line to dominate – most notably the CART series in North America, their top single-seater class – and notch up five successive wins to 1987 in the celebrated Indianapolis 500. This, then, is no oily-rag team sneaking in through the Formula One tradesmen's entrance, but one which feels the time is ripe for a renewed onslaught on what is still considered the pinnacle of motor-racing.

The man on whose shoulders this heavy responsibility rests is Ian Phillips, a former journalist whose lifelong devotion to motor-racing has earned him the dubious reward of running a Formula One team – one which he has enjoyed to the full. 'That first year was great,' he laughs. 'We were slightly disappointed to finish where we did, but then we're an ambitious lot so we were bound to be . . . We set out to re-establish ourselves and gain respectability – and with two class wins in the category I think we achieved that aim without enjoying the results we deserved. At Adelaide, for example, we were lying sixth and looking realistically at fourth when Ivan Capelli had that spin; twice we didn't finish because of rotor-arm failure; and several times we didn't make it because of a recurrent problem over piston rings in our engines. I don't think there was ever a non-finish you could put down to poor preparation.'

The refreshing thing about Phillips and the March garage – one of the further-flung outposts of Grand Prix empire, well down the pit lane from the Williamses and McLarens of this world – is the lack of verbiage. Ask a simple question and a straight answer is what you get. 'We got caught out by our own naïvety,' admits Phillips. 'The engine thing is a case in point: by the time we'd wrung it out of the specialist builder that the piston package was wrong, we'd lost five engines, and that was leaving it a little late. The major lesson we learned, therefore, was that you have to be wholly in control of every aspect of your effort. It's the only way to create a World Championship team.' Fair enough, but is that realistic? 'We'll have a bloody good go at it!' is the wholly characteristic reply. In 1987, though, when the March team unwrapped a new engine to find oil pouring out of its ports as soon as it went on the test bed, we were literally talking of oily rags . . .

Speaking of engines – which, as they say, we shall a bit later – Phillips was not guilty of naïvety when he got in first with a request for the Judd

Opposite *Ivan Capelli in the 1987 March. New boy Mauricio Gugelmin* (inset left) *eyes up his March drive for 1988*

Inset right *March mastermind Robin Herd CBE*

normally-aspirated 3.5-litre engines which will be used by three teams in 1988 as the sport prepares for a return to non-turbo power the following year. This team may be better equipped than most, by virtue of its name, to steal a march on the opposition, but how did Ian pull off that little coup? 'Three days after we opened our doors in January 1987, John Judd told me he was doing this engine. Could we fit a dual engine mount, as March cars so often do for the various categories we run in, and test for him in July? The answer was yes. But at Spa we faced an engine crisis of the kind we mentioned earlier. John was there for the Formula 3000 race, so I asked him how soon we could have one of his new engines. He said he needed Honda's permission to do it [Judd has long-standing associations with the Japanese manufacturer in other formulae and was building a unit based on a Honda block], so I went and got it for him; I called them on the Saturday and he got the go-ahead on the Sunday.'

Even so, life was not a bed of roses. 'We had planned racing with the Judd engine for the last three rounds of the Championship, but it got a little behind, and we're now looking forward to using it in 1988. To me, John is the best engine builder in the world as far as preparation is concerned – and the great thing is you can talk to the guy, unlike the situation we found ourselves in last year! All right, we may still be at a disadvantage in qualifying against the turbos, but I think in the races there will be nothing in it at all. Our ambition is to qualify in the top ten and race in the top six, and if we don't do that we shall all be very disappointed.'

No oily-rag outfit this, either, when it comes to resources in both money and personnel. March has increased its workforce from fifteen to fifty-five since re-entering GP racing last year, and Phillips sees designer Adrian Newey as one of the most significant newcomers. 'Adrian is our Technical Director, and I believe within three years he will be seen as *the* bright individual in Formula One. We also have our own CAD system, and unlike some teams I could mention I think we are using it the right way. Even before we went Grand Prix racing we had a couple of people fully versed in its use, and now we have trained more so that we are utilising some sixty per cent of its enormous powers – whereas other teams have had such systems for years and still don't know a quarter of what they can do.'

Part of the Phillips enthusiasm is based on solid financial backing from the Tokyo-based Leyton House company, the leisure-wear branch of a Far Eastern conglomerate with wide-ranging interests. 'They committed to us very early,' explains Ian, 'and we know they're with us until the end of 1989 at least, with all the security that gives us. Our global budget for the coming season is of the order of ten million dollars . . . We will have a separate test team this year, something we couldn't manage last year

John Judd: smiling despite the strain of supplying three teams in 1988

because of the tightness of the schedule – it just wasn't possible to get the car back to the works and turn it around in time. The race team itself won't be much bigger, but we have our own electronics department, a separate sub-assembly for engines, gearboxes and rear suspensions, and generally the strength to run two cars as we will be doing in 1988.'

Not for March the troubles with 'star wars' between drivers that tend to develop elsewhere. Italian Ivan Capelli, nicknamed Dustin Hoffman because of his film-star looks, already enjoys a good working relationship with new recruit, Brazilian Mauricio Gugelmin. 'We took Mauricio to Japan to meet the sponsors and the team in working conditions,' reports Phillips, 'and the two got on very well. We shall have (fingers crossed!) a new car ready for the first Rio test – we got the first chassis on 29 January – and though the car may not be complete when we put it on that plane it will be there! Not only that, but I think it's going to be a bit of a trendsetter.'

Phillips' last remarks, interestingly enough, concern the running of the sport as he has seen it from the inside in his first year. 'It was thoroughly enjoyable,' he reflects. 'I've never enjoyed a year's work so much in my life. And I must say that I have a higher regard now for Mr Ecclestone than I did before, when it was high enough. He is the only man with a vision of the future for Formula One, and the sport just has to be controlled by him. He looks beyond tomorrow: if Bernie has made a good living out of Grand Prix racing, I have no quarrel with that – he has made it possible for lots of other people to make a good living too.' As our next chapter concerns precisely that Mr Ecclestone, the President of the Formula One Constructors' Association, we must thank Ian for the cue . . .

2 NO ROOM AT THE TOP?

He may only be shoulder-high to most people, but he is motor-racing's Mister Big. He even says himself that some people refer to him as the sport's Godfather. But in reality he is only the President.

Bernie Ecclestone is President of the Formula One Constructors' Association, the organisation that looks after the interests of most of the teams on the GP circus. It is a role that, in the past, has brought him into conflict with the sport's governing body, the Fédération Internationale de l'Automobile. Today there is a truce between Mr Ecclestone and Monsieur Balestre, the President of La Fédération Internationale du Sport Automobile, the organisation described quaintly by the FIA in its own year book as its 'sporting ministry'. How has peace broken out? Quite simply France's Jean-Marie Balestre has invited Britain's Bernie Ecclestone to become a FISA vice-president with special responsibility for the selling of the sport – to television, to sponsors, to just about anyone who can bring in the money, be it English pounds, French francs or American dollars – although Swiss francs would be preferable, please. And judging by millionaire Ecclestone's past, bringing in the money is just one of the things he does best.

Ecclestone is not immediately an easy man to talk with. Dapper in razor-sharp black slacks, sparkling white open-neck shirt and peering from behind tinted glasses, he darts around the pits and paddock before disappearing into his inner sanctum, the black and silver FOCA motor home complete with leather upholstery, thick-pile carpet and, again, the obligatory tinted glass – Ecclestone can see you outside, but you can't see Ecclestone inside. If the media enjoy spinning the web of mystery about FOCA's President, there is more than a hint that the man at the centre of everybody's attraction secretly revels in his reputation.

Bernard Ecclestone was born in Suffolk fifty-seven years ago, later moving with his family to Bexleyheath. 'I studied for a BSc in chemical engineering,' he says today. 'My parents thought it was a good thing to study the subject. I had no interest in that as a career, though.'

Above *Bernie Ecclestone: king of Formula 1*

Right *Ecclestone* (left) with FISA president Jean-Marie Balestre: harmony at last?

What he was interested in was his hobby – buying and selling second-hand motor-cycles – something he had been doing as a teenager, long before he studied (it's alleged he quit before his finals) and found himself boringly working in a laboratory after the last war. His hobby became his work and after buying out his partner in a local garage he quickly built up his business to become the third-biggest motor-cycle dealer in the country – and a rich man. But at the same time as selling two-wheel machines he was riding them – around Brands Hatch. What price would Ecclestone pay for a piece of the motor-cycle GP action when the British race is run for the first time at Brands in 1989? Indeed FOCA could well be looking after the television interests of motor-cycling in the future.

Top *A movable feast: the FOCA bus . . .*

Bottom *. . . and its palatial interior*

It was back in those heady post-war days that Ecclestone laid the foundation for his FOCA empire today. He had progressed into single-seater 500cc racing cars, competing against the equally youthful Stirling Moss and Peter Collins. After crashing at Brands he decided his future was not going to be from inside the cockpit but rather from outside, and when he recognised the potential of a friend, Stuart Lewis-Evans, he became his mentor. The managerial motor-racing bug had bitten and Ecclestone was on his way.

In 1958 Lewis-Evans was killed in a Vanwall during the Moroccan GP at Casablanca. The death of his friend took the edge off Ecclestone's motor-racing appetite for a while, so he made even more money in the property boom of the 1960s. But racing was in his blood and, after managing the affairs of the Austrian driver Jochen Rindt until he too was killed (in practice for the Italian GP in 1970), he bought the Brabham racing team. It was the winter of 1971 and the way ahead was clear.

During Ecclestone's leadership at Brabham, from 1972 up to the end of 1987, they took part in 243 races, and won the World Championship in 1981 and 1983 with Nelson Piquet (see p. 173). If one of your drivers has won the world title twice in sixteen years you might feel some glow of satisfaction; indeed, most of Brabham's competitors might envy the Chessington-based constructor. But in truth Brabham has not performed nearly as well as the top teams. There has been no world title for the marque and only twenty-two wins. By contrast, in the same period, Ferrari have won forty-five races, six constructors' titles and three drivers' titles; McLaren have won fifty-one races, three constructors' titles and five drivers' titles; Lotus have won thirty-seven races, three constructors' titles and two drivers' titles; and Williams in three years less, 1975–87, have won forty races, four constructors' titles and three drivers' titles.

But Ecclestone is philosophical about it all. 'This is a funny business,' he says. 'I've run Brabham for the last I-don't-know-how-many years out of my own money. Not once has Brabham ever been able to stand on its own feet with the amount of sponsorship money we've been given. I've always tried to keep a very up-market type of sponsor that's not controversial in any kind of way. They're a nice, virginal type of people – Parmalat with dairy products and Olivetti [computers]. We've tried to toe the line a little bit. It's because people, like television companies, complain there are too many cigarette companies involved. We try to make life a bit easier to run a team and put the effort in that I need to make the team successful.'

Does Ecclestone have any doubts? It seems he may have. 'You have to be a lunatic to be in the business for a start,' he insists. 'No sane person would want to run a race team. The amount of effort you put in and the

Above *Business as usual: one phone is never enough*

Left *Early days on the Brabham pit wall*

Top *Adelaide 1987: king of F1 with kingpin driver Nelson Piquet, the new World Champion*

Bottom *Good old days? Piquet in the 1983 Brabham that powered him to his second world title*

amount of risks you take – you wouldn't want to do it unless you are a racer. There are plenty of other businesses.' It all comes back to money, though, as the Brabham boss is quick to point out. 'The more you give a team the more they spend to win. If you increase the budget of, say, Frank Williams – if you doubled his budget, at the end of the year his balance sheet would be exactly the same. He would find a way of spending the money. He would have a bigger wind tunnel, more cars and more staff.

'It takes perhaps £20 million a year to run a two-car team. It may be unreal money to the man in the street . . . it's unreal money to the man out of the street . . . it's unreal money to me. My budgets are not as big as that. That's what I'm saying. I've got to go out and hustle. You can't relate to it. For example, someone's working all their life for a small percentage of what a race driver gets for one season. The funny thing is that it's not worth anything to be a world champion from, say, Nelson Piquet's point of view. He's got existing contracts so he probably wouldn't get any more money for being world champion.'

So with an expensive and not totally successful team to run it was no surprise when Brabham announced that they would not be competing in 1988. With his increasing involvement in FOCA and FISA, and with his personal bank balance backing up Brabham, Ecclestone seemed to have had enough. 'I need to neglect all that I do for racing worldwide and find somebody else to do that and then run Brabham – or find somebody else to run Brabham and I can look after the other side of things . . . or maybe not run Brabham for a year or two. Contrary to general opinion I don't have any ambitions. What I like to do is get up in the morning – and go home at night and think that I've done a good job. I've always tried to do the best I can do whatever I am doing, whether I was delivering newspapers or gardening or running what I'm doing. I like to get job satisfaction; to have done the best that I can do. That's the problem, because I take things on, I'm totally committed. So what seems to be a good idea at the time ends up with me being totally involved.'

Now most acquaintances of Ecclestone could no more see him *actually* delivering newspapers or gardening than flying to the moon. It is obvious, though, that he sees his future increasingly in the running of the sport worldwide – if that were more possible in his case. But it seems he is happy to be number two – or is he? 'I wouldn't like to be President of FIA or FISA because I'm one of the boys. I started this part of my life with a race team down there with the racers. I'm still trying to look after the racers and therefore look after the sport. The new position I've been given is to look after the commercial and promotional affairs of the FIA, which effectively isn't so much in the politics of the Federation but more in trying to perfect the sport.'

While Ecclestone sees himself more as a diplomat, there is no doubting he is a good politician as well. But what are FOCA and FISA all about? Is Ecclestone the sport's Godfather? FISA, it is worth recalling, was formed as far back as 1922 and makes the law concerning international motor sport and sees that it is enforced. It has, coincidentally, in sixty-five years of existence, had only six presidents – a Swiss, a German, two Belgians and two Frenchmen – significantly, never an Englishman. Much later, in the early seventies when Ecclestone was establishing himself at Brabham *and* as a force to be reckoned with in the increasingly commercial motor-racing world, the British teams, which made up most of the field, formed the Formula One Constructors' Association, to look after their interests in general and, at that time, their travel arrangements in particular. Ecclestone was their man and a few years later took the title President. The slumbering FISA did not realise its control of the sport would never be the same again. Ecclestone, with the best brains in the business all British, if not with the tradition of the French and Italians, now wielded the power and the purse strings. It was only when Jean-Marie Balestre, the former French Resistance hero, took over the reins of FISA in 1978 that war broke out between the two organisations, a war that is now only really turning to peace with Ecclestone having more than a foot in both camps.

Back in 1981 the uneasy FISA/FOCA marriage was on the point of divorce. Balestre wanted to wrest virtually all negotiating rights from Ecclestone, who not only refused but actually ran the South African GP that year under the FOCA banner and minus those teams with allegiances to FISA. The separation had begun. (Incidentally, that race at Kyalami is not recognised as an official World Championship GP and broke a 14-year run of South African races. Ironically the drivers returned there for only four more official races – 1982–5 – before politics persuaded the sport South Africa was not a good place to race in.)

After the 1981 race common sense prevailed, and following a public, at least, reconciliation the warring factions decided to make a go of the marriage, signing a Concorde Agreement which gave Ecclestone almost what he wanted – the rights for FOCA to negotiate contracts and distribute the monies – and a nice personal commission for the FOCA President himself.

Ecclestone again: 'Early on, when I started FOCA, it was all a bit of a mystery. It was the English against the Continentals. They said the English were trying to write all the rules to win all the races. It was the English mafia – and I was the Godfather. It went on from there and those kind of

Opposite *The controversial 1981 South African GP: Carlos Reutemann's Williams leads*

The legendary Jean Behra is incidental as the picture shows trackside advertising has always been a GP feature

stories circulated the world. It's not until you come into contact with people and they frisk you, they see you haven't got a gun stowed away in your pocket and all those funny things. Lots of people meet me and say, "My God, you're totally different to what I expected." ' As far as his wealth is concerned he says mischievously: 'People say I organised the train robbery! If that's what people want to believe, so what!'

There's no question of a robbery when he comes to selling a GP, however. Just sound commercial sense and dozens of different deals being completed – with television, with advertisers, with sponsors, with race-tracks, with circuit stallholders, with airlines, with hotels, with just about anyone who wants a slice of the action (and thousands do) and who can swell motor-racing's already bulging coffers. The key, though, is television. Without about one and a half hours' coverage of each of sixteen races worldwide, who would want to sponsor a race (the Shell Oils British GP), advertise at trackside (Goodyear, Lucas, Dunlop), sponsor a car (Canon, Data General) or even buy a team (Benetton – formerly the Toleman marque)? And those 25-plus hours do not include the two official practice days that precede race day or the tyre-testing days, which are often televised, as well as the countless news stories that the sport generates.

FOCA, acting of course on FISA's behalf as well as its own, is mid-way through one enormous deal – a six-year arrangement with the European Broadcasting Union, which counts the BBC amongst its members. How the BBC came to be transmitting Formula One in sound as well as on television was well documented in the *BBC Grand Prix* book published in

1986. In fact 1988 marks the tenth anniversary of BBC Television's return to coverage of the World Championship, after previously sporadic broadcasts had dried up completely when sponsors and advertisers, realising the tremendous potential of 'moving billboards', became a little too greedy in their demands for awareness. The television authorities were more than a little sensitive at that time – remember the Durex Surtees?

In fact, regardless of the sponsorship of a car or the event, the agreement with the EBU, let alone others that FOCA may have with non-European broadcasters, devotes much time and space to the question of advertising at race circuits. FOCA guarantees that advertising will 'not affect the quality of the coverage or interfere with a complete and aesthetically satisfying view of the races for the television audience'. Potential advertisers are made well aware of the rules before they commit themselves to small fortunes. There should be, for example:

- no advertising between the cameras and the race
- no advertising on the surface of the circuit
- no luminous, rotating or fluorescent signs
- no mobile banners, pennants, etc.

Above all, no advertising should break the rules of the country in which the race takes place. And that means heavy additional restrictions, for example, on tobacco advertising in countries such as West Germany, Canada and Great Britain. In practice that means, in the United Kingdom, tobacco companies may not have banners closer than a quarter of a mile to each other, and that cars, drivers, mechanics and all potential wearers of tobacco advertising cover up when the cameras roll. Of course, if there is no broadcast or if the advertising is out of camera range, the host broadcaster does not object. And just to quieten the objectors, those broadcasters who do have tobacco restrictions on advertising in their own countries obviously do not have any sway in those countries which do not have such rigid rules. That is why you will see Marlboro, Camel, Gitanes and West quite clearly on cars and men in, say, France or Italy.

Just how seriously FOCA takes the question of advertising is made clear in sections of its EBU contract where it agrees to provide a complete list of advertisers before each race for vetting, and further agrees to reduce by one-third the not-inconsiderable sum the EBU pays for a race if there is an infringement or even gives the EBU the opportunity to withdraw completely from the broadcast with no payment being made. In fact FOCA employs an agency to police the advertising at the circuits.

Just how powerful a medium television is, and how important it has become to the sport of motor-racing, is shown conclusively by statistics

compiled by FOCA from figures supplied by the world's broadcasters. The sixteen races were watched on television, live or deferred, by 1,449,316,000 viewers in fifty-two countries – that is, each race was watched, on average, by between 90 and 91 million armchair addicts. It is estimated that 68,987 minutes of race action alone were screened – or nearly 48 days! And the figures don't include news broadcasts or other additional transmissions. No wonder there is little shortage of sponsors wanting a slice of the action if it involves a successful car and driver always 'in the frame'.

Most of the fifty-two countries took television coverage of all sixteen races, ranging from the unlikely outposts of Costa Rica and El Salvador to the Lebanon and Nicaragua. But three – Bulgaria, Kuwait and Russia – transmitted only one race – not surprisingly Hungary, the race that Mansell claimed cost him the world title when a wheel-nut flew off his car. The British race, for reasons best known to themselves, was also not taken in Czechoslovakia, Denmark, Greece, Yugoslavia and the Ivory Coast. The most popular Grand Prix, surprisingly, was Mexico – with a total audience of 109,111,000, easily beating Japan (100,822,000), San Marino (97,135,000) and the old favourite Monaco (95,556,000).

All the television figures show increases over the previous year (see p. 174), but there are those who believe Ecclestone's preoccupation with the medium works to the detriment of the paying spectator. He himself will have none of it. 'Television has created more public interest in motor-racing, better than other sport because racing is so exciting, with so many different aspects that perhaps other sports do not have – the colour, the glamour, a little bit of danger, a bit of everything. It's a natural. I mean, if somebody wrote a film he couldn't have written it better than when Lauda and Prost battled it out in 1984 to finish with only half a point between them; or when Prost, Mansell and Piquet went to Australia [in 1986] and the tyre exploded. If somebody brought a story-line to you and read it you would say, "Go away and please try to write something a little more likely because this is all a bit of a joke." It even happened through-out 1987 with Nigel and Nelson, ending with Mansell's crash in practice for the penultimate race of the season in Japan. The sport would be 100 per cent worse off without television. All sport would be worse off without television. There is nothing bad about television in sport.'

To be fair, not everyone would agree with that sentiment – particularly those who yearn for the good old days of British Racing Green when The Sport was king and commercialisation was not. How they must have loathed the sight of cars attempting to drive round the concrete blocks

Opposite Spot the driver (Mansell) among the commercials . . .

that made up a so-called circuit in the car park of Caesar's Palace in Las Vegas – or the almost-as-bizarre scenario of the world's top drivers competing in Dallas under the uncomprehending eyes of Bobby Ewing and family from the American soap opera.

For the old school the proof was in the pudding: Las Vegas lasted for two races (1981–2) and Dallas for just one (1984). But for Ecclestone the events were right: staged in eye-catching places where television, and the rest of the world's media, would provide the publicity and the sponsors would come flocking. The more hype, the more publicity, the more money. Ecclestone is motor-racing's Barnum and Bailey – and as he plots new circuits – Dubai, Moscow, Peking, who knows – he says he doesn't give a fig for yesteryear.

'I think those days were terrible compared to what we have today. It was totally disorganised – just a good old club. You know – a lot of mates all got together and if the public came along and viewed, good. But they didn't. Most of the people in motor sport then were reasonably well off and were racing to entertain themselves. They weren't professionals. All sport now is a full-time job.'

Ecclestone doesn't need a second chance to warm to his task. 'I think that we [FOCA] have put more sport into motor-racing than there is any other so-called sport, and there's more left in Formula One than in most of the other areas. For a start we've got something totally out of our control – we've got men *and* machines, whereas most other sports don't fall into that category. We don't seed people. We don't select people and say you can run and you can't run and all that nonsense. If you can get the job done you can be in Formula One – which is more than you can say for lots of other sports.'

How does he answer his critics who say the sport is a predictable procession with the financially favoured few always at the front? 'Look, if there were twenty-six drivers starting the race with exactly the same car, one would be first and one would be last. There's no such thing in this world as equal. Some drivers will get the best out of their machinery and themselves in different ways and different circumstances. The same guy would keep winning and the same guy would keep coming last because they would not be equal. The drivers that win are the guys who've got enough brains to get themselves into cars that can win. I would have my doubts that Fangio was the best driver in the world but he won more World Championships because he was the man in the right car at the right moment.'

But Ecclestone almost contradicts himself when reflecting on the 1987 World Champion, Nelson Piquet, the driver who won the first two of his three World Championship titles driving for Brabham – and

Ecclestone. 'I don't think he was a worthy World Champion in 1987 because he won only three races to Nigel Mansell's six. But he got the required number of points. He played the system. Maybe if the system had been different Nelson would have won six races. He didn't need to. I'm sure Nelson knew what he had to do although I don't think that was the case, incidentally, when Keke Rosberg won the Championship in 1982 with only one win that season.'

Mike Hawthorn won his World Championship in 1958 with just one victory, but managed four pole positions and five fastest laps compared with Rosberg's single victory, one pole position and no fastest laps – the worst record of all thirty-eight World Champions. But, as Ecclestone would have it, he played the system. And so, in every way, does Ecclestone. He runs on engine oil, not blood, and the world of motor-racing should be thankful he's on their side.

He is the most influential single figure in the sport and he is something of a mystery man until you can get behind the veneer – but only a little way. Those newspaper journalists who have made it to his industrial estate-based FOCA and Motor Racing Development organisation (the Brabham holding company), in the London backwater of Chessington,

Left *Finest showman of them all: Keke Rosberg after topping the bill at Las Vegas, flanked by Elio de Angelis (left) and René Arnoux*

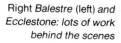

Right *Balestre* (left) *and Ecclestone: lots of work behind the scenes*

have homed in on the obligatory paper shredder, the German-registered Mercedes 500SEL parked in the reserved space, the private Lear jet at Biggin Hill, the still cellophane-wrapped oriental ivories at the luxury two-storey Thames-side penthouse where Frank Sinatra once lived, although nowadays Ecclestone and his family no longer live there, even though he apparently continues to own it.

Indeed, one probing gossip columnist did nothing to endear herself to the man she described as a 'mysterious motor-racing tycoon' by revealing that he has splashed out £7 million on Adnan Khashoggi's former nine-storey Knightsbridge home – and is paying another £2 million converting the prestigious Princes Gate address. It is said that Ecclestone, his second wife, beautiful Yugoslav model Slavica, and their young daughter Tamara will eventually share the tower block – complete with eighth-floor swimming pool – with FOCA personnel when Ecclestone decides to move part of his business interests out of Chessington. Indeed, some of his Brabham employees, with time on their hands as the team's future hung in the balance before he pulled out of the 1988 season, were thought to be working, not on Motor Racing Developments, but at a certain Knightsbridge address. Why shouldn't they? This is Bernie Ecclestone. He deserves the last word.

On the future: 'I don't think the sport is anywhere near its peak as regards making it professional – not as a way of making money but for the television viewer and the fans at the circuits. I want to give the best value, the best show.'

On making money: 'I think people that work to make money are idiots, complete idiots . . . they never have enough time to spend the money anyway. I'm wealthy inasmuch as I have generated enough money to do what I want to do . . . but very little of what I want to do is personal.'

On doing something else: 'Anything. I don't really mind. All businesses are the same really and truly, aren't they? You've got to buy cheap and sell dear and keep the costs down. I'd like to own the zoo [the nearby Chessington Zoo]. I could go in there at weekends – as an inmate!'

On himself: 'I'd probably hate it if I tried to analyse myself. I try to be honest with people . . . straightforward and fair and give the best I can. I trust people until I find out otherwise and I'm generally all right because most people are honest.'

On his punishing, self-imposed 14-hours-a-day, 365-days-a-year schedule: 'The good thing about it really is you never know what's going to happen because it's such a volatile sort of business. When I arrive in the morning I don't know what's going to happen. If I knew I probably wouldn't be here. I enjoy the hassle. I enjoy everything I do, otherwise I wouldn't do it. I do what I do because I like it.'

3 *CIRCUIT JUDGE*

Like ordinary human beings, GP drivers have their preferences – they like certain cars, they like those cars to be set up in a certain way, which is always a function of the circuit on which they are being required to perform.

In this chapter we look at the tracks that make up the modern GP calendar. From the street circuits of Monaco or Detroit to the spectacular settings of Spa or Rio, these differ almost as much as do the drivers themselves. To help set the scene, British drivers Nigel Mansell, Derek Warwick and Jonathan Palmer pick out features that would have to be included in their ideal circuit, while World Champion Nelson Piquet and others also have a word to say here and there.

All of us have favourite motor-racing venues, either because of the characteristics of the circuit itself, or because it stirs happy – or unhappy – memories. In the last analysis, however, the driver himself – the man who puts his life on the line for seventy laps or so of any given track – is the man most qualified to set himself up as circuit judge . . .

Monaco: the most recognisable circuit of all

Brazil

Autodromo Nelson Piquet
Baixada de Jacarepaguá

Circuit length: 3.126 miles/5.031 km

Race distance: 61 laps, 190.692 miles/306.891 km

Lap record: Nelson Piquet, 120.305 mph/193.607 kph (1986)

Flat but quick, Rio is notable for the fervour of the locals – usually split between Senna and Piquet – and the heat. As Mansell says, 'Rio is always a tough one to start the year with because of the heat, and because it's an anti-clockwise circuit.' Last year's winner was Prost (McLaren). For Warwick, Jacarepaguá is a track to enjoy: 'Long, fast corners – a place I really like.' Rio is also where close-season testing stops and the teams find out how much good it has done . . .

San Marino

Autodromo Dino Ferrari
Imola

Circuit length: 3.132 miles/5.04 km

Race distance: 59 laps, 185.3 miles/ 297.36 km

Lap record: Nelson Piquet, 127.151 mph/204.631 kph (1986)

Conveniently 'relocated' so that Italy may enjoy two GPs in the year, the Autodromo Dino Ferrari is named after Enzo Ferrari's son and is one of the spiritual homes of his team. Set in lovely countryside with a variety of turns and straights, popular with most of the drivers. Winner in 1987, Mansell (Williams) says: 'Imola is a very demanding circuit: hard on brakes, because there are a couple of really high-speed sections followed closely by sharp corners.'

Monaco

Circuit de Monaco
Monte Carlo

Circuit length: 2.068 miles/3.328 km

Race distance: 78 laps, 161.298 miles/259.584 km

Lap record: Alain Prost, 85.957 mph/ 138.335 kph (1986)

The showcase race of any season, with the most trying working conditions for teams and journalists. 'I'm the sort of driver who can adapt to differing circuits,' says Warwick, 'and Monaco is a very special sort of challenge.' As for Palmer, the Swimming Pool section near the harbour, and the stretch that passes by the famous Casino, would feature in his ideal track. Senna (Lotus) won in 1987.

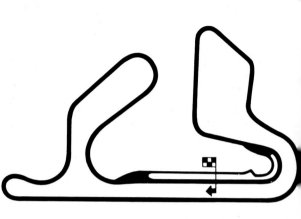

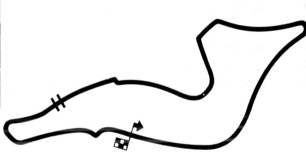

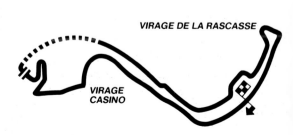

VIRAGE DE LA RASCASSE

VIRAGE CASINO

Mexico

Autodromo Hermanos Rodriguez
Magdalena Mixhuca, Mexico City

Circuit length: 2.747 miles/4.421 km

Race distance: 68 laps, 186.8 miles/
300.628 km

Lap record: Nelson Piquet, 124.974
mph/201.127 kph (1987)

Named in memory of Mexico's
famous racing brothers Pedro and
Ricardo, this is the proverbial track of
two halves. A fast right-hander
slingshots the drivers on to a long pit
straight, with a demanding series of
turns on the far side of the circuit –
what Palmer calls 'a lovely left–right
sequence after that long straight'. It
was also a race of two halves in 1987
– Mansell (Williams) took the honours
after a restart.

Canada

Circuit Gilles Villeneuve
Montreal

Circuit length: 2.756 miles/4.435 km

Race distance: 69 laps, 190.182
miles/306.06 km

Lap record: Nelson Piquet, 115.456
mph/185.808 kph (1986)

Named after the great French-
Canadian racer, and set on an island in
the St Lawrence River, this is another
track much loved by all who go there.
Winner in 1986 (not on the 1987
calendar): Mansell (Williams). Piquet
likes Montreal: 'The track is nice to
race on: what I'd call a good mixture of
a street circuit and a permanent track.
And it's quick . . . Canadian
spectators, too, are very
knowledgeable and almost as fanatical
as the Italians – but less noisy!'

United States

Detroit Grand Prix Circuit
Detroit, Michigan

Circuit length: 2.5 miles/4.023 km

Race distance: 63 laps, 157.5 miles/
253.471 km

Lap record: Ayrton Senna, 89.584
mph/144.171 kph (1987)

Least appealing of the street circuits,
Motown is bumpy and very demanding on cars and drivers. Dominated by
the imposing Renaissance Center,
symbol of the city's revival. Senna
(Lotus) proved his street-fighting
qualities with a fine win there in 1987.
In Piquet's view, 'You need a well-
balanced car which is very responsive
around all those tight turns and in and
out of the narrow sections. The margin
for error around the concrete-walled
track is virtually zero.'

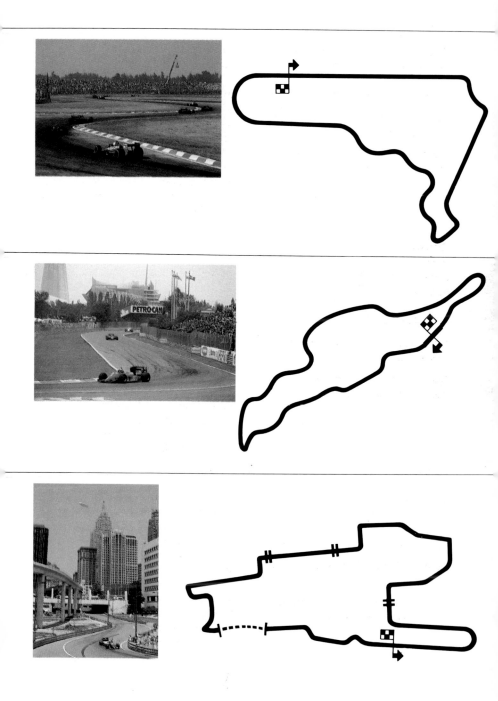

France

ASA Paul Ricard
near Marseilles

Circuit length: 2.369 miles/3.813 km

Race distance: 80 laps, 189.543 miles/305.04 km

Lap record: Nelson Piquet, 122.641 mph/197.372 kph (1987)

'A rather special track,' in Mansell's words, 'and much better for the modifications made in 1986,' the Circuit Paul Ricard is one of the few purpose-built GP facilities. Set high in the arid scrubland of Provence, the sun-baked track features the Mistral Straight, one of the longest and quickest on the calendar. A favourite for test sessions when England is cold and wet . . . The 1987 winner: Mansell (Williams).

Great Britain

Silverstone Grand Prix Circuit
near Towcester, Northants

Circuit length: 2.969 miles/4.778 km

Race distance: 65 laps, 192.985 miles/310.579 km

Lap record: Nigel Mansell, 153.059 mph/246.325 kph (1987)

Scene of the first-ever World Championship GP, Silverstone, for some, has been emasculated by the addition of chicanes that attempt to slow cars coming on to the pit straight. For Palmer, the corners named Club and Stowe would feature on a composite circuit, but Warwick feels rather differently. 'Silverstone gives me very little satisfaction. The circuit is flat, boring for spectators, and to my mind on the dangerous side for drivers.' Mansell (Williams) won in 1987 with a remarkable overtaking manoeuvre to beat team-mate Piquet.

Germany

Hockenheimring
near Heidelberg

Circuit length: 4.223 miles/6.797 km

Race distance: 44 laps, 185.83 miles/299.068 km

Lap record: Nigel Mansell, 143.823 mph/231.462 kph (1987)

Unfortunately famous as the track that claimed Jim Clark's life in 1968, Hockenheim has some long, flat-out curves and a curious infield Stadium section with packed grandstands. 'Difficult to set the car up for,' was Mansell's comment. The 1987 winner: Piquet (Williams).

LIGNE DROITE DU MISTRAL

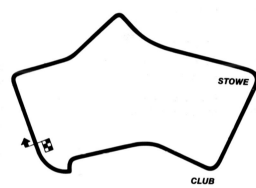

STOWE

CLUB

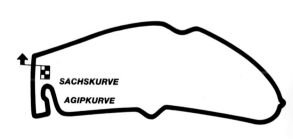

SACHSKURVE

AGIPKURVE

Hungary

Hungaroring
Mogyoród, Budapest

Circuit length: 2.495 miles/4.013 km

Race distance: 76 laps, 189.557 miles/305.064 km

Lap record: Nelson Piquet, 99.602 mph/160.295 kph (1987)

Introduced in 1986 and an immediate hit, though some of the drivers found the twisty section after the pit straight rather overdone. Winner in 1987 was Piquet (Williams), for whom 'Hungary is a nice design, but very dirty at first – like Mexico, it was a new circuit.'

Belgium

Circuit de Spa-Francorchamps
Francorchamps

Circuit length: 4.312 miles/6.94 km

Race distance: 43 laps, 185.429 miles/298.42 km

Lap record: Alain Prost, 132.513 mph/213.260 kph (1987)

One of the great motor-racing shrines, even if it now bears little resemblance to the 14-kilometre challenge that daunted the great names of the past. Set in the wooded hills of the Ardennes, it boasts the fearsome Eau Rouge, where the cars speed down the old pit straight, turn left–right, and at the same time face a steep surge up the hill into a left-hander. 'No doubt about this one,' says Palmer. 'Eau Rouge would have to be on anyone's all-time favourite list of outstanding features.' Prost (McLaren) won in 1987 after a restart.

Italy

Autodromo Nazionale di Monza
near Milan

Circuit length: 3.604 miles/5.8 km

Race distance: 50 laps, 180.197 miles/290.0 km

Lap record: Ayrton Senna, 149.479 mph/240.564 kph (1987)

Ferrari's other home, no longer the ferocious banked circuit that set high-speed records, but still a daunting combination of long, quick straights and slowing chicanes. 'I'd take from Monza the curves called first and second Lesmos,' enthuses Palmer. The 1987 race fell to Piquet (Williams). For Mansell, 'Monza is unique in the way it attracts so many people and so much attention.' The marshalling, he believes, is a bit suspect: 'I'll never forget the year when I came out of the last corner and found the pit straight full of people!'

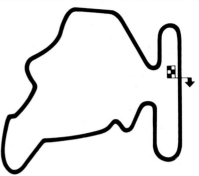

EAU ROUGE

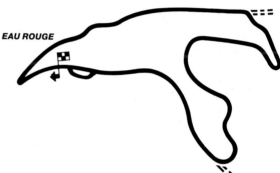

CURVA PARABOLICA

CURVE DI LESMO

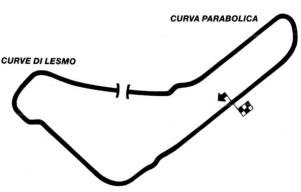

Portugal

Autodromo do Estoril

Circuit length: 2.703 miles/4.35 km

Race distance: 70 laps, 189.207 miles/304.5 km

Lap record: Gerhard Berger, 122.737 mph/197.526 kph (1987)

Mansell calls this 'a driver's circuit, with a variety of fast and medium corners as well as some nice straights'. For Palmer, 'There are a couple of right-handers just after the start–finish line I'd like to keep in my ideal circuit.' In 1987 Prost (McLaren) not only won the race, but in so doing beat Jackie Stewart's all-time record with his 28th GP victory. 'A very exciting circuit,' says Piquet, 'which puts the emphasis on the driver as much as on the car. There is no chance to relax at any point . . .'

Spain

Circuito de Jerez
Jerez de la Frontera

Circuit length: 2.621 miles/4.218 km

Race distance: 72 laps, 188.708 miles/303.696 km

Lap record: Gerhard Berger, 108.47 mph/174.566 kph (1987)

Nice track, shame about the location. Built with regional government assistance to bolster the economy of the sherry-growing region, the circuit would do so if anybody ever went there. Smallest crowds in the calendar, for what was – in 1986, at least – the closest race of all, Senna beating Mansell by fourteen-thousandths of a second.The 1987 winner was Mansell (Williams), and Palmer would retain 'all the quick bits' for his composite circuit.

Japan

International Racing Course
Suzuka Circuit
Suzuka, Shiroko

Circuit length: 3.641 miles/5.859 km

Race distance: 51 laps, 185.67 miles/298.809 km

Lap record: Alain Prost, 126.21 mph/203.116 kph (1987)

Purpose-built facility inaugurated in 1987, the winner being Berger (Ferrari). It was also the scene of Mansell's painful practice accident that ended his season and, for the second year running, his title ambitions. No doubts in Palmer's mind: 'Suzuka is the best circuit on the calendar now; it's got sweeping corners, on an undulating track that manages not to be too bumpy. I was very impressed.'

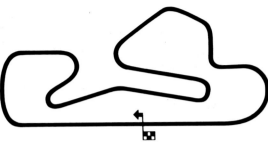

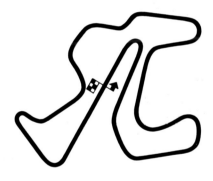

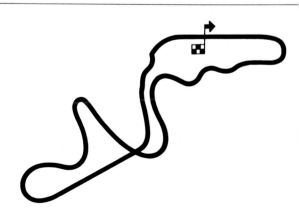

Australia

Adelaide Grand Prix Circuit
Adelaide, South Australia

Circuit length: 2.347 miles/3.777 km

Race distance: 82 laps, 192.454 miles/309.796 km

Lap record: Gerhard Berger, 105.123 mph/169.175 kph (1987)

The slogan 'Adelaide Alive' was coined when this street circuit took the World Championship down under, and the city has lived up to it. An instant hit with drivers, even if team manager Frank Williams calls it 'desperately hard on cars', Adelaide also had the audacity to earn the title of best-run race in the 1985 calendar when it first came on. Scene of Mansell's dramatic tyre failure in 1986, it saw Berger give Ferrari a second consecutive victory at the end of 1987.

Austria

Österreichring
near Knittelfeld

Circuit length: 3.692 miles/5.942 km

Race distance: 52 laps, 191.993 miles/308.984 km

Lap record: Nigel Mansell, 150.5 mph/242.2 kph (1987)

With Spa, the most beautiful of all the circuits, even if its narrow pit straight and the resultant mayhem at the start of the 1987 race have made it a non-starter for this season. In Palmer's eyes, it's a question of 'biting the bullet', as he puts it, and including the ultra-quick right-hander called the Boschkurve. 'A bit of a test, that,' he muses, as he builds it into the ideal circuit. The twice-restarted 1987 race went to Mansell (Williams), who made his GP debut here in 1980. 'A fantastic track', in the opinion of Williams' Chief Designer Patrick Head. 'With one exception, all the corners are very fast and the emphasis is on a well-balanced car. Aerodynamics and fine tuning are important, and it's essential that the minimum load is placed on the tyres.'

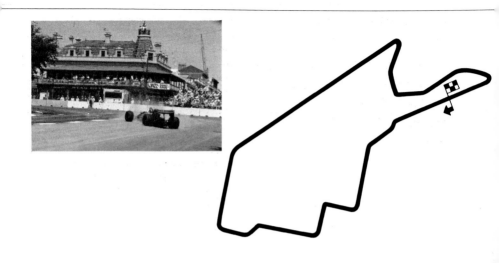

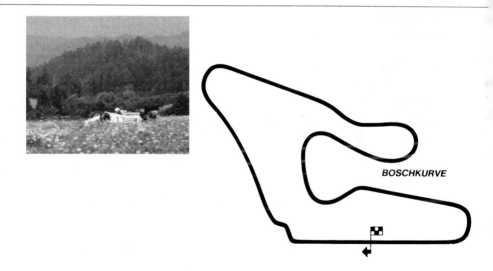

BOSCHKURVE

Great Britain

Brands Hatch Circuits Ltd
Fawkham, near Dartford, Kent

Circuit length: 2.614 miles/4.206 km

Race distance: 75 laps, 196.05 miles/
315.503 km

Lap record: Nigel Mansell, 135.22
mph/217.569 kph (1986)

Brands Hatch. No, not a double-take –
we just don't know if the Kent circuit
will again alternate with Silverstone
next year. Quite different, in that it
swoops and bends through
undulating countryside, with
marvellous viewing facilities and a
series of challenges to driving skill.
And Warwick particularly likes one
corner: 'I love Paddock Bend – it's
really exhilarating, provided you get it
right! It's one spot that always gives
you a buzz . . .' Last winner here:
Mansell (Williams) in 1986, when the
two Williams cars lapped the rest,
including Prost.

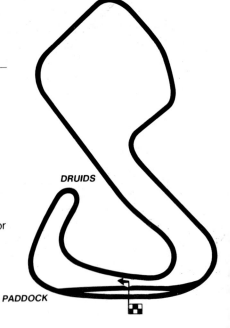

Last word to Derek Warwick as well.
'I can't agree with Jonathan about
Suzuka, which really didn't make all
that much of an impression on me. For
me the best of the lot is Rio: Brazil at
the very start of the season when it's
all getting under way again, and it's
hot, and there are all those long, fast
turns . . . I think Brazil has a lot to
offer!'

4 TRACK RECORD

While the preceding chapter dealt in brief with the circuits on today's GP calendar, this section takes a closer look at the rules and regulations governing the running of a GP on a particular track – and at the people whose responsibility it is to ensure the safety of all concerned, whether it be the spectators who flock in their hundreds of thousands to watch Formula One, the mechanics working under intense pressure in crowded pit lanes, or of course the men who put their lives most obviously on the line: the drivers.

To point up the dangers involved, let us look back on some of the incidents that marred the 1987 season and brought unwelcome attention to this aspect of the sport. The most dramatic of these occurred at the Austrian GP, and has had unfortunate repercussions for its organisers.

When you are sitting in a 200-mph vehicle with little between you and the surrounding world, it can be of little comfort to see concrete walls in close proximity. At many GPs such walls are commonplace, and of course the start/finish line at every race lies beyond the pit wall, the refuge and working area for other members of the team. The magnificent Zeltweg circuit, or Österreichring, as it is better known, has a particularly narrow pit straight, with forbidding walls on either side. GP grids are closely staggered along the straight, the Noah's Ark principle of two by two applying, except that each 'row' of the grid in fact sees the slower car slightly behind its faster partner. Nonetheless, the potential for disaster when twenty-six high-speed racers are waiting to outdrag one another into the first corner is high.

Anyone doubting the veracity of that remark need look only at the British GP of 1986, when Jacques Laffite's F1 career was ended by a multiple pile-up at the very first corner, Paddock Bend. Austria 1987 was to bring further distressing proof of the perils these men face each time the red light switches to green. In the jockeying for position, such bumping and barging ensued that the race was restarted, not once, but twice: chaos was the order of the day, if the expression is not too Irish, and

Above *Traffic jam at Zeltweg, 1987: Fabre on top for once!*

Right *Victim of Brands Hatch pile-up: Jacques Laffite*

Ferrari's Michele Alboreto for one was so incensed by the incidents and the danger they created that he was seen in the hottest possible conversation with the representatives of the sport's ruling body. Curiously enough, the race itself – edition number three – boasted a high number of finishers, not always the case in the 1987 season. But FISA issued an edict requesting changes to the circuit if it was to retain its WC status for 1988, so that it seemed likely that Zeltweg – a magnificent track of ups and downs, twists and turns – had lost the GP for the coming season. All the more mysterious, then, that it should be deemed

Top *Local hero Gerhard Berger at an unhappy Zeltweg*

Bottom *Second problem spot: who is facing the right way at Estoril 1987?*

appropriate for F3000 cars to race there, but that is another question.

As if Zeltweg were not bad enough, we then had Estoril, scene of the 1987 Portuguese GP. Once again there was first-lap mayhem – not at the start but on the first corner. Piquet's Williams and Alboreto's Ferrari laid claim to the same stretch of tarmac, which was unfortunately big enough for one car only. The inevitable coming-together occurred, and the net result was some eight or nine Formula One cars in a bunch, not one of them facing in the same direction as any of the others. Leaders Mansell and Berger, of course, had long vanished into the Portuguese countryside, and this is the aspect that makes the incident so terrifying.

Over to Martin Brundle, whose Zakspeed was one of the victims in the accident. 'I was out of the car, and making my way back by the shortest route to the pits to see what could be done, never imagining that the race would not have been stopped as soon as the severity of the incident was noted. I was walking back, as calm as one can be in such circumstances, when I found a Grand Prix coming towards me . . .' There had, in fact, been no red flag to stop the race, and Messrs Mansell and Berger, with Prost in close attendance, were already on lap 2. Only the experience and quick reactions of some of the most senior drivers saved the situation, but to be in the Williams pit when Mansell returned – the race duly stopped – was to see a GP driver's temper very close to breaking-point. The Estoril incident highlights the vital importance of the marshals' role to which we must return.

Austria, Estoril . . . and Monza, another track to receive a FISA warning about its facilities for 1988. It may be the simple fact that Monza is the home of the world's most fanatical Formula One followers that throws one particular aspect of modern GP racing into sharp focus, but its pit lane holds too many terrors for too many people. Narrow in the extreme, in stark contrast to the generous pit straight beyond the wall, it becomes the most crowded pit lane on the calendar: sponsors, sponsors' guests, public relations personnel, the working press whose right to be there is beyond question, cameramen, photographers – and a host of hangers-on whose combined presence makes life a nightmare for crews trying to work on cars and for drivers who bring them into the pits. For these chaps, 80 mph is slow, but it would make a severe dent in any human frame that got in its way – especially when they are so often giving to switching off and coasting down the pit lane to their respective garages. In the circumstances, it is astonishing that no major pit-lane incident has occurred recently, and alas only a matter of time before it does . . .

Each of these examples serves only to emphasise the dangers attendant upon motor-racing. Go to any track, anywhere, and you sign a waiver, or by buying a ticket agree to specific conditions, which effec-

Monza's pit lane is the most overpopulated in modern GP racing

tively protect the organisers from any claim in the event of injury. 'Motor-racing is dangerous' is the phrase that begins the wording, and the fact is undeniable. What can be done, what indeed has been done, to improve this aspect of the sport in an era that has seen the ingenuity of the boffins defeat all artificial restraints upon the performance, i.e. the sheer speed, of GP cars?

One crucial development has been the introduction, as a universal protection, of the celebrated 'Armco' barriers that now circumscribe the circuits of the world. There are those who claim that Jim Clark would not have died had Hockenheim, in 1968, been equipped with Armco along the stretch where Clark's car snapped sideways and made ferocious impact with the trees. One function of the safety inspectors at a given track, though, is to ensure that the barriers are effectively bolted and stable throughout their length, that overlaps lie in the right direction – away from that of the cars' arrival – and that such complementary structures as catch fencing are in place. Too many have been the occasions on which a car, or parts thereof, have flown into the crowd with tragic effect . . . and there is no need to go into them here.

One man whose work takes him closer than anyone else to the heart of safety matters is Professor Sid Watkins, the London neurosurgeon who oversees Formula One medical facilities. 'Prof', as everyone fondly knows him, has been a full-time official in GP racing since 1978, but for some sixteen years before that he was associated with the United States GP at Watkins Glen, and with the British round of the World Championship from 1970 onwards. He joined the RAC medical commission as its neurosurgical adviser in 1970, is still adviser to FOCA, and is President of the FISA Medical Commission.

What, then, are the Prof's responsibilities? 'Oh, enormous' comes the breezy answer. 'First of all, I have to inspect medical facilities at the circuits and the rescue arrangements, and approve rescue plans; and I have to make sure the Chief Medical Officer and his team have made appropriate arrangements for the evacuation of casualties to hospital or to specialised units if necessary.' His achievements in this respect are just as enormous, though he can recall a day when it was not so. For instance, one man who blazed a trail in matters medical in motor-racing was BRM's Louis Stanley who – in conjunction with the Grand Prix Drivers' Association – made provision for a specialist mobile unit of hospital standard to be on hand at racing circuits.

'I remember it well,' says the Prof. 'The Stanley passion wagon we

Opposite *René Arnoux inspects the armco: first start, Austria 1987*

Inset *Armco in action: a safe height for all?*

Medical monarch: Prof Watkins on duty
Inset Mansell, Prost and wheelchair, Hungary 1987

called it, and a splendid thing it was. But people did not accept it: doctors felt it too high-powered, and when it came to races outside Britain we couldn't always take our own medical team because their qualifications would not be recognised locally. They even used to ignore it at the British Grand Prix until I started running it . . .'

Circuits all over the world have now followed the route Stanley and his like were trying to lay down, one which gives Professor Watkins cause for justifiable pride. 'Some places we go to needed, shall we say, a little more encouragement than others to put their medical house in order, but the facilities you will find now at any Grand Prix track are first-class. Our own at Silverstone and Brands Hatch are good examples; at Brands, we used to have to take the poor chaps under the grandstand, forcing our way through all the concession stalls and so on, while at Silverstone we used to have just a wooden hut. Now both circuits have medical units offering the standard of care you would expect from a first-rate intensive care unit.The same can be said of Germany, of course, but also of new tracks like Jerez and Hungary.'

The Prof's input, indeed, to new facilities on the GP calendar is crucial, the Hungaroring being a case in point. The medical commission – or, to save time, the Prof himself – has to approve the plans for medical provision at the planning stage of a circuit itself, Budapest's purpose-built track being the latest example. As the sport has grown and prospered, what developments in medical care have pleased him most?

'Undoubtedly the acceptance of the concept that resuscitation takes place within the car' is the immediate reply. 'And extrication of an injured driver is based on a judgement as to whether doing so will further endanger his life or exacerbate his injuries. Added to which we now have provision for a rapid car with all possible facilities to go to the scene of any accident, which in turn depends on good radio communication and an alert Clerk of the Course – something, alas, we don't always have.'

Someone very close to the centre of GP medicine is Dr Rowland Cottingham, a London anaesthetist who devotes much of his spare time to the BRSCC, spends one weekend in three at a race-track in this country or abroad, and finds time after his 'proper' job in intensive care at Harefield Hospital to think long and hard about levels of care in F1. 'The modern history of motor-racing medicine', explains 'Rowly', 'may be traced to a battered old green van that started to appear at Brands Hatch in the mid-sixties. This unprepossessing vehicle, scrounged from a competitor for a very small sum, was the forerunner of the modern highly-equipped rescue vehicle. General concern had been voiced, not so much over the quality of assistance provided as over the speed of response. The chief fire marshal, a doctor and a couple of helpers armed with crow-

Above *Sand trap catches out Andrea De Cesaris*

OFFICIAL PACE CAR

Right *Ready to go: Prof in the pace car*

bars crouched in the rear of this asthmatic machine that would wheeze into life to deliver the contained experts to the site of the problem.'

Help was on hand, however, from a giant corporation whose contribution to motor sport, in Britain as elsewhere, has been immense. 'In 1968 Ford offered a Transit van, which was then kitted out with fire extinguishers, cutting equipment and medical emergency supplies and registered as an ambulance. The level of sophistication of this vehicle, complete with silver fireproof suits and two-way short-wave radio, means it can be termed the first true Rescue Unit.'

Dr Cottingham has seen new safety measures such as the Armco and catch fencing – designed to dissipate the energy of a fast-moving car in

This is why: De Cesaris in his most spectacular accident in the Ligier – as seen on TV

stretching the links of a chain fence as it crashed through several layers – improve the safety record of the world's circuits, but contemporary measures, he believes, take things a stage further. 'New circuits (Hungaroring, the new Nürburgring) have been specifically designed with constant-radius curves less likely to unsettle cars, and leading to huge run-off areas; old tyres have been carefully arranged in strapped-up piles in front of the Armco to act as huge shock absorbers; and catch fencing has largely vanished to be replaced by sand traps – actually areas covered by a specific size of pebble, and a stroke of genius. A car sliding off the track falls into the trap; its wheels sink in, and the car is brought to a rapid but extraordinarily gentle stop. Both car and driver, although possibly a little sand-blasted, are uninjured, and what could have been an extremely serious accident may cost nothing more than two minutes brushing the pebbles off.' It is such innovations, coupled with the enormous strides in developing lightweight, rigid materials to construct safety cells around drivers, that have so dramatically reduced the injury toll in Formula One.

No less important, as Dr Cottingham concludes, is the sheer scale of aid now readily on hand at a major incident. 'Formula One is unique in

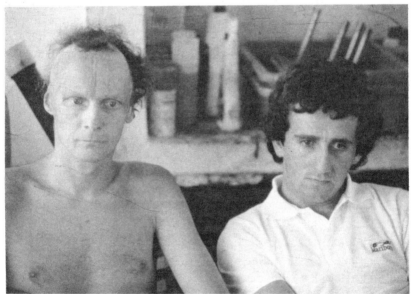

Top *At the heart of the action: marshals ponder the mysteries of the Portuguese false start*

Bottom *Scars of battle: Niki Lauda (left) with his former McLaren team-mate Alain Prost*

sport in this country in being able to get ten Rescue Units and their doctors as well as several fast-response cars and *their* doctors, all volunteer specialists in such emergencies, to the scene of an incident within three minutes. A doctor will have arrived on foot within thirty seconds; radio messages will have flashed over the emergency channels from Incident Officers in constant touch with the circuit nerve centre, Race Control. Within seconds crews will be on stand-by, and then scrambled to the incident in a carefully planned sequence of responses practised during every major race meeting. They will start arriving moments later, some of the faster ones actually overtaking the Formula One cars as they slow down; each will park in such a way as to offer maximum protection from any race traffic still on the circuit.' And that is only the first wave of response, in an overall strategy that can make as many as fifty doctors – collected from marshals' posts around the circuit – available.

No sport, as we have said before, sees its participants so close to the limits of survival with such sustained intensity, and inevitably Professor Watkins remembers incidents that have left a particular mark even on this most experienced man. 'All the deaths, of course, are hard to take, especially if it's very clearly a fatal accident on the circuit and not something that takes its final toll a few days later. I was especially saddened, I suppose, by the death of Gilles Villeneuve, and although it was not a fatal accident I was very sorry to see that pile-up at the British Grand Prix that ended Jacques Laffite's career just when he was set to break the all-time record for Grand Prix starts.' Like everyone connected with motor-racing, the Prof tries hard to resist the natural urge to get close to the drivers, knowing full well the price such friendships may exact. 'I don't avoid such contact, of course,' he explains, 'but let's say I make it my practice not to hang around any particular teams, or use their motor homes: I try to keep a certain distance, as we all do, within the context of what is a very close-knit community.'

Professor Watkins is possibly the most respected member of that community, even if his work confines him to certain areas of the track at certain times of the day – always ready to respond to a given situation. Not the least of his attributes is a sense of humour, allied to his wealth of experience, that makes him one of the sport's great raconteurs. To balance the sadnesses of motor-racing, he has a fund of stories to underline its humorous side. 'I suppose the funniest thing I've ever seen,' he recalls with a chuckle, 'was two or three years ago in Brazil when we had a first-lap incident to go to and the local doctor who was with me lost his false teeth in the bottom of the car. No great tragedy in itself, but it was one of those vehicles that had had everything stripped out but the barest essentials, and the floor was covered in that oily gunge they use as sealant or whatever. Anyway, the teeth turned up – but they were all blackened and messed up by this stuff – and he popped them straight back in! Funniest thing of all was that he was wearing a crash helmet – I don't know how the hell they got out in the first place!'

The Prof's serious comments are more pertinent at a time when the last two seasons have seen the loss of Elio de Angelis, killed in Lotus-testing at Paul Ricard, and the accident to Jacques Laffite as well as major 1987 'shunts' for Nelson Piquet at Imola and Nigel Mansell in Japan. Besides men like Watkins, however, there is another band of individuals whose role in all forms of motor sport, but most visibly in Formula One, is crucial.

All sport is a matter of teamwork. A GP driver in the cockpit at 200 mph and more may be entitled to feel somewhat isolated, but he knows – when he has time to think about it – that his work is the culmination of a team effort taking in the work of, literally, hundreds of people. Apart from those who put cars on grids in the first place, the most important team at any motor race is the marshals. Their role has been highlighted by occasions both tragic and heartwarming, and the British, it would appear, are the best of the bunch.

To put their work in context, think back on two incidents only. In 1976 Niki Lauda, then World Champion, expressed concern about the safety of the celebrated Nürburgring in Germany. Covering no less than 22 kilometres of the Eifel Mountains, the Ring could not possibly be policed by a large enough number of marshals to guarantee the safety of drivers should any accident occur. By a curious coincidence, it was Lauda himself who suffered when his Ferrari crashed and, despite the heroic efforts of fellow-drivers who stopped and dragged him from the burning wreckage, he was severely scarred and even given the last rites before an act of the most extraordinary will-power brought him back to life and top-level competition. A year later, further tragedy: the promising Tom Pryce, a rare and natural talent, was killed at Kyalami in South Africa when inexperienced marshals ran across the track to attend a minor incident and were confronted by Pryce's Ensign hurtling over the brow of the hill. One marshal made it, but the other was hampered by a fire extinguisher which caught the hapless Pryce and killed him – and the marshal – instantly. There is no joy in dwelling on such moments, merely the need to underline the – literally – vital role the marshals play. What do marshals do, how do they become marshals in the first place, and how are they equipped to cope with this demanding job?

Mike Oxlade is National Public Relations Officer for the British Motor Racing Marshals' Club, or BMRMC as it is better known. 'We have something over 2000 marshals in motor-racing in this country, all of them volunteers. The reasons we are so highly thought of in this area are threefold. Firstly, we have so many meetings – six or seven across the land on an average weekend – that our trainees can quickly amass a tremendous amount of experience. In fact, the average time spent by each of our members in marshalling last year was around twelve days. Then there is the grading scheme that applies, and the training involved in each step up the ladder. It will normally take a novice two years to become a fully-fledged marshal, three to four years for such work as specialist rescue, and to become a top-line official or observer, up to six years' work under constant supervision. And last but not least is the fact we have already mentioned, that they are all volunteers – so we can take their commitment and dedication almost for granted.'

As the BMRMC's booklets set out in several pages of carefully-worded information, the training levels and grading scheme are paramount: from course marshal, responsible for circuit inspection (oil, mud, stones and so on) and reporting to the observer, to fire or incident marshal, to flag marshal with responsibility for giving the often life-saving signals to drivers bearing down at 180 mph, and so on to Incident Officer or Observer – 'the eyes and ears of the Clerk of the Course', as the literature puts it. 'If you are a good marshal,' claims the BMRMC, 'you will probably be at the scene first, or at least a very close second,' a statement endorsed by one of the volunteer marshals at the last British GP.

Marshals in action again: first on the scene of Nigel Mansell's Suzuka crash, 1987
Inset BMRMC – safety matters

Simon was a 24-year-old foreign-exchange dealer from London (funny the people you meet at motor-racing) who had gone through the selection process observed before the premier event in the country's motor sport calendar: volunteering through his club, who forward their own selections to the RAC, overlord of all motor sport in Britain, for approval. 'It's a tremendous honour to be here today,' enthused Simon, who had arrived at Silverstone on the Friday, nipped away for a wedding, and was back for duty on race day itself at around seven in the morning. His attitude to the risks involved was simple: 'It's amazing how fast you can react when you see something happen. You first assess how much danger you want to put yourself in, but then as the adrenalin flows something else takes over – for example, you find yourself picking up equipment so heavy you wouldn't dream of lifting it otherwise, and you go and do your job.'

Another of Simon's remarks points up the appeal of marshalling. 'I'd really like to do some motor-racing myself, but it's just too expensive at the moment.' Mike Oxlade agrees: 'Marshalling, we believe, is an excellent route into motor sport for the genuine enthusiast. There are no hard and fast rules on the degree of commitment we expect, and of course there are no restrictions on grounds of gender – women account for some ten or fifteen per cent of our membership.' Not that there are any great rewards – not even expenses, in many cases – and the best perk of the job is that you are offered cost-price specialist clothing such as the bright orange fireproof overalls that are the uniform of the modern marshal. A snip at £22 . . .

Teamwork is the name of the game: the recommendations in the booklets always emphasise the chain of command, the need for constant vigilance and coolness, and the willingness to subject personal whim or impulse to the greater needs of overall discipline. On the lighter side, one of the more practical instructions to budding marshals is 'Do not pack your food in a paper carrier bag'; refreshments, like people, can fall victim to the vagaries of the British climate! But seriously, camaraderie is the essential reward in Mike Oxlade's eyes: 'It is very much teamwork, marshalling, and the great thing about it is the variety of people you meet. Doctors, dustmen, bank clerks and all sorts go in for the job, but there is no pecking order except within the framework of our grading scheme. We're all the same and we all have one aim in mind: the safety of all concerned at a motor race.'

Whatever the secret, British marshals are much in demand at overseas events, especially the nearer Continental races such as Spa or Monaco. 'We regularly take groups of fifty or sixty marshals to those races,' adds Oxlade, 'but they go on their own ticket. Quite often the foreign organisers do not even pay expenses, so our people pay their own fares, look after their own accommodation, and generally just get on with it.' It is this spirit, perhaps, allied to the expertise already described, that sees British officials invited to make recommendations at overseas circuits – the new Hungaroring, for instance, scene of the first World Championship GP behind the Iron Curtain in 1986, called on British expertise in marshal matters as well as on the medical front.

'We have been asked to help in the setting up of similar organisations all over the world,' Oxlade goes on. 'A few years ago we ran a race in Dubai; our officers have been invited to South Africa and Israel; and at the time of this conversation two of them are actually in India giving advice to our budding counterparts there.' There could scarcely be a higher compliment to the British system than this international demand, though Oxlade is quick to point out that other countries have their own very high standards as well. 'West Germany is very good, though their approach is rather different from ours. We tend to rely on the guys on the bank to get in quickly and do the job, with the specialist vehicles as back-up, while the Germans put the emphasis very much on the specialist vehicles, with the "ordinary" marshals in support.'

The marshal then – whatever his grade – is a vital element in the successful running of a GP. Once the powers that be have stipulated the layout of the track, his job is to assist drivers who find difficulty in coping with it, whether in minor incidents such as harmless spins or in cases where a man's life may depend upon a split-second reaction. No wonder we all gasp when we see pictures such as those of Streiff's Tyrrell in flames at the 1986 French GP – and no wonder there was universal condemnation when the marshals, alongside whose fire post Streiff had been careful to park the stricken vehicle, failed to respond immediately. Not only was what should have been a relatively small turbo fire allowed to turn into a major incident, but the comedy of errors saw foam gush out of the wrong end of the fire tender that eventually did arrive – after coming the wrong way down the pit lane. On a high-speed circuit such as Ricard, the potential for disaster was almost too great to contemplate.

Pity, too, the marshal who becomes the victim of a driver's frustrations, as was the case in Mexico last season when Ayrton Senna's Lotus became immobilised on the track. No matter how eloquently the Brazilian might gesticulate to the contrary, the men on the spot were adamant that he could not be restarted but must be pushed off the track. Once resigned to the fact, Senna was out of the cockpit in a flash to vent his spleen on the luckless marshal, not verbally but with considerable physical force, before stalking off in the direction of the pits. Who wanted thanks anyway?

Joking apart, these moments are the down side of the marshal's work. They are overwhelmingly outnumbered by those nameless, unremembered acts of minor – and major – heroism that help keep cars on the track, drivers intact inside them, and the spectacle of GP racing as refreshingly incident-free as, in the last few seasons, it has been. 'A marshal', says the BMRMC booklet, 'has a degree of insanity in his make-up.' Maybe so, but it is surely a fine madness that makes such people give so freely of themselves for the good of a sport they love. If, incidentally, you wish further information about marshals and marshalling, the man to write to is Ken James, Secretary of the BMRMC, at 2 Temple Close, Bletchley, Milton Keynes. But remember: 'On becoming a marshal, spectating ceases . . .'

What they have to contend with: what's left of the Tyrrells after first-lap crash, Spa 1987

Not all circuits are under such watchful eyes as Monaco . . .

5 POWER GAMES

One of the most telling incidents of the 1987 GP season took place at a circuit which has seen its share of controversy over the years, but this time it was not Monza's celebrated chicanes and straights that staged the drama. The world's press were invited, during the weekend of the Italian GP, to a conference in the park surrounding the celebrated tarmac. It was to prove the rather embarrassing climax to a weekend in which the race itself, for all its considerable interest at a crucial stage in the destiny of the World Championship, was virtually eclipsed by a blizzard of press releases and statements all relating to just one thing: the power behind the GP winners.

What happened, first of all, was that the Williams team, who have bene-fited since the last race of 1983 from use of the all-powerful Honda engine, formally announced what had been bruited around the paddock for some time: the Japanese manufacturer was withdrawing from its con-tract in order to supply not only Lotus (for whom they had been providing engines in 1987) but also McLaren, previously users of the TAG-Porsche unit. The rationale behind this move, was presented somewhat differ-ently by the two parties, Honda and Williams Grand Prix Engineering, and brought into sharp focus the power games that lie at the very heart of the modern GP empire.

Frank Williams himself spoke of a 'divorce' after what had been one of the happiest and closest marriages in Formula One: did not Honda, after all, have their own engine facility in the Williams plant at Didcot? The con-ference in the park was called by Honda, partly to put a more favourable gloss on their own release, received with unanimous hostility by the press, British first and foremost, and to introduce the new driver partner-ship that would carry the Honda flag for McLaren. As this duo included both the world's most respected and outstanding driver, Alain Prost, and the brilliant and ambitious Brazilian Ayrton Senna, a certain degree of interest was generated . . . However hard the Japanese hierarchy, assembled before the world's top Formula One writers, and their public

Above left *Final touch: keeping Honda polished*

Above right *The power behind Williams – but not in 1988*

Right *Telling tales: the Monza press releases*

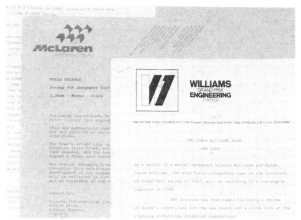

relations army tried to explain their sudden decision to break the Williams contract, it was obvious from the sheer electricity in the Monza air that the listeners felt something underhand was happening. The move aroused controversy that may well spread and become increasingly bitter as the teams fight for survival in the sudden absence of turbo engines and the concomitant scramble for normally-aspirated units – which will take over the Formula completely again from the start of 1989.

Whatever the reasons for this divorce, the Monza affair merely highlighted the arguments going on in the GP world at that time. Why, in the first place, was the turbocharged era coming to an end? Would the return of atmospheric engines make the sport any less costly, or bring it back closer into line with what we understand as 'ordinary' motoring? Was this further evidence of the fact that there rarely has been, and perhaps never will be, a genuinely stable Formula One?

Before attempting to answer these and other related questions, it may be useful to describe – purely in layman's terms – the differences between a naturally-aspirated engine and its turbocharged competitor. By 'natural aspiration' is understood the process by which air enters an internal-combustion engine through the regular suction stroke in its cylinders. By 'supercharging' (of which the turbocharger is a refinement) is meant, in the words of one standard text, 'the admittance into the cylinders of an engine of an air charge larger than what the cylinder would obtain as the result of the regular suction stroke'.

The changes in Formula One since the inception of the World Championship in 1950 have been largely to do with engine capacity, and the advent of turbocharging in 1977 was French car-giant Renault's attempt to increase the power output of a GP engine within the regulations set down by FISA. From 1966 (the 'return of power' we spoke of briefly in the first *BBC Grand Prix* book) these allowed for either engines of 1.5 litres with supercharging or 3.0 litres 'unblown'. That 1988 sees the eighth modification in these rules, and that 1989 will bring in yet another, is neither here nor there for our present purposes.

As distinct from the superchargers familiar on such legendary cars as the 'blower' Bentleys of between the wars, the turbocharger is not driven directly by the engine it is serving. Instead, it derives its energy from the exhaust gases, which are channelled into the driving of a turbine, another – if high-speed – form of compressor to blow air into the engine. Such are the speeds attained by the turbine vanes and the temperature of the compressed air generated that this has to be passed through an intercooler before entering the engine if it is not to do so with explosive effect; hence, in part at least, the modern GP car design with those large sidepods that exist partly to house the intercoolers themselves.

The turbocharger, now standard on a number of road-going family cars, exists to increase the efficiency of the engine by enhancing the fuel–air mixture and thus the power output. As we have seen before, Renault used it to claim the first turbocharged victory in modern Formula One, aptly enough at Dijon in the French GP of 1979 in the hands of French driver Jean-Pierre Jabouille. Renault would go on to claim a further fourteen World Championship race wins, but their failure to secure the championship itself and their subsequent retreat is now part of GP

Turbo temperatures can run high, as on De Cesaris's Brabham

Inset *Jean-Pierre Jabouille wins in the turbocharged Renault at Dijon in 1979*

history, if still a source of no little puzzlement to those who observed it all.

It would be instructive, if rather tedious, to list the occasions on which 'turbo failure' had been used as the reason (excuse?) for failures by drivers or their teams in the decade since Renault brought the device into the sport. No armchair fan can have failed to pick up the countless occasions on which the clouds of smoke gushing from the back of a car have been explained by Murray Walker or James Hunt as yet another turbo fire, usually more spectacular than they are actually dangerous. But it is sobering to recall the huge fire that engulfed Philippe Streiff's Tyrrell at the Paul Ricard circuit soon after he had brought it to a halt with turbo failure in 1986, or the point so dramatically made by a frustrated Michele Alboreto when he brought his blazing Ferrari down the pit lane at Brands Hatch in the same season's British GP.

A mixed blessing, then, these turbocharger things? Fair comment, perhaps, but the banning of atmospheric engines for the 1986 season was a pragmatic recognition, by the powers that be, of the great divide that had opened up between the turbocharged teams and their non-turbo competitors. As if to prove the point, the gulf could scarcely have been more obvious than in the 1987 season that saw a return to a mixed Formula: 1.5 litres supercharged or 3.5 litres unblown. That gulf can be summed up in one formulation: the generation of raw power. For in 1987 the discrepancy between what a turbocharged engine – the Honda behind Mansell and Piquet, the TAG-Porsche propelling Prost and Johansson, the Ford units in the Benettons of Fabi and Boutsen – can do and the output of the non-turbocharged units – in such cars as the Tyrrells, Larrousse Lolas and March – was actually written into the rulebooks themselves when FISA decided that 1987 would contain not one but two World Championships in each category.

To take cognisance of the power divide, the non-turbo teams would compete for their own title, with drivers of such cars also bidding for glory in their own category. Inevitably, these became known as second-division stuff, though there were times when both cars and drivers would surprise their more powerful brothers and sisters. But the mere fact that a Colin Chapman Trophy (for cars) and a Jim Clark Cup (for drivers) were brought into being underlines the acceptance by all concerned that competition was no longer taking place on equal terms, and this is one of the strands of thinking behind the move to bring uniformity back.

At some circuits in 1987 the gap between, say, pole position and the best practice time recorded by a normally-aspirated car could be almost unbelievable. Throughout the season the turbocharged cars could run at a maximum of 4.0 bar, that is, at an engine pressure of four atmospheres: the air–fuel mixture taken into the cylinder was increased, the efficiency and power output of the engine thereby multiplied. This, we must repeat, is no new phenomenon in the GP world: from the early days, and particularly in the ultra-competitive thirties, supercharged cars screamed away from their 'unblown' rivals. What is new in recent years is the sheer power generated, something like 6000cc for the typical turbo team of 1987. Since the naturally-aspirated cars were struggling along with some 3500cc to play with, it is scarcely surprising that they came to be seen on several circuits as a form of mobile chicane that was just one more irritant for drivers of turbocharged racers.

Not that the 4.0-bar figure was the norm: such high-rate running would have brought the drivers up against two intriguing features of the turbo era, namely the pop-off valve and the over-rapid consumption of fuel. The pop-off valve, made universal on turbocharged cars by FISA edict at the start of 1987, is, in the delightful words of leading GP writer Nigel Roebuck, a device which 'works on the same principle as a condom acceptable to Rome', in this instance allowing just enough compressed air to enter the engine but not permitting an overdose that might have overproductive results . . . Having set the limit to four atmospheres for 1987, the sport's governors have decided on a 2.5 maximum for 1988, with a fuel limitation of 150 litres for each race (reduced from 195 litres in 1987). This gives further pause for thought on the possibility of increased embarrassment to those who thirst for turbo power. With around 200 laps to cover, the spectacle of some of the greatest racers – Prost, perhaps most obviously – being forced to slow right down and zig-zag their

Shell Oils

BRITISH GRAND PRIX
SILVERSTONE
10-11-12 JULY 1987

FIA FORMULA 1 WORLD CHAMPIONSHIP

Issued by RAC MSA Race Services

```
            1987 FIA FORMULA ONE WORLD CHAMPIONSHIP
          SHELL OILS BRITISH GRAND PRIX - SILVERSTONE

    COMPUTER OLIVETTI                    LONGINES TIMING

               OFFICIAL PRACTICES TIMES
```

POS	NUM	DRIVER	NAT	CAR	1st SESSION B.TIME LAP	2nd SESSION B.TIME LAP	Mph
1	6	N.PIQUET	BRA	CANON WILLIAMS-HONDA	1'07.596 19	1'07.110* 15	159.267
2	5	N.MANSELL	GBR	CANON WILLIAMS-HONDA	1'07.725 11	1'07.180* 9	159.101
3	12	A.SENNA	BRA	CAMEL LOTUS HONDA	1'09.255 5	1'08.181* 16	156.765
4	1	A.PROST	FRA	MARLBORO MC LAREN TAG	1'08.577* 5	1'09.492 8	155.060
5	20	T.BOUTSEN	BEL	BENETTON FORD	1'09.724 10	1'08.972* 15	154.967
6	19	T.FABI	ITA	BENETTON FORD	1'10.264 6	1'09.244* 4	154.394
7	27	M.ALBORETO	ITA	FERRARI	1'10.441 9	1'09.274* 19	154.272
8	28	G.BERGER	AUT	FERRARI	1'10.328 8	1'09.400* 14	153.994
9	8	A.DE CESARIS	ITA	BRABHAM BMW	1'10.787 15	1'09.435* 11	153.845
10	2	S.JOHANSSON	SWE	MARLBORO MC LAREN TAG	1'10.242 7	1'09.541* 13	153.699
11	7	R.PATRESE	ITA	BRABHAM BMW	1'10.012* 16	1'10.020 16	152.665
12	11	S.NAKAJIMA	JPN	CAMEL LOTUS HONDA	1'10.619* 16	1'10.996 9	151.353
13	17	D.WARWICK	GBR	U.S.F.& G.ARROWS MEGATRON	1'10.654* 7	1'10.701 20	151.270
14	18	E.CHEEVER	USA	U.S.F.& G.ARROWS MEGATRON	1'11.053* 6	1'11.310 18	150.427
15	24	A.NANNINI	ITA	MINARDI MOTORI MODERNI	1'13.737 3	1'12.293* 19	147.848
16	25	R.ARNOUX	FRA	LIGIER LOTO MEGATRON	1'12.503 5	1'12.402* 19	147.626
17	9	M.BRUNDLE	GBR	WEST ZAKSPEED	1'12.052 6	1'12.632* 4	147.150
18	10	C.DANNER	GRD	WEST ZAKSPEED	1'15.033 2	1'13.337* 5	145.744
19	23	A.CAMPOS	SPA	MINARDI MOTORI MODERNI	1'15.719 2	1'13.793* 10	144.843
20	21	A.CAFFI	ITA	LANDIS & GYR/OSELLA A.R.	1'18.495 6	1'15.550* 8	141.440
21	30	P.ALLIOT	FRA	LARROUSSE LOLA FORD	1'14.770 20	1'15.868* 10	140.882
22	4	P.STREIFF	FRA	COURTAULDS TYRRELL FORD	1'17.200 15	1'16.524* 12	139.874
23	3	J.PALMER	GBR	COURTAULDS TYRRELL FORD	1'16.644* 22	1'17.105 10	139.455

The figures say it all: huge gaps between top turbos and leading naturally-aspirated cars

cars to slosh the last drops of fuel into a thirsty engine has become one of the most frequent and most ironic in Formula One. Is this true GP racing, we have asked ourselves, or the type of exercise that belongs more properly to the very different world of endurance racing?

The 1988 regulations may, then, bring about a reduction in performance, as the boost level available to turbo teams will be limited to 2.5 bar. With an estimated output of 3750cc, this cuts dramatically the advantage they enjoy over the non-turbo teams – so much so that Frank Williams, in the wake of his losing Honda power, was heard to opine that some of the 1988 races might well be within the grasp of teams with naturally-aspirated power units. As if to lend credence to this English team manager's views, no less a force than Ferrari were seen to be hesitating, in the off-season between 1987 and 1988, over their decision on running with 2.5-bar turbo units or atmospheric engines, and Maranello driver Michele Alboreto was reported to have had a quiet smile on his face after testing with the naturally-aspirated unit.

Fuel supplies choked off even further, then, and a mere 2.5 bar of boost to fool around with. Who said the days when drivers were dictated to by the myriad gadgets in their cockpits had come to an end? Speaking

Boutsen and Benetton: quick but brittle in 1987

of which, drivers themselves may now be the crucial contributors when it comes to separating the race winners from the also-rans. If the Formula is again virtually uniform – and it will be from the start of 1989 – then it is surely the skills of the man behind the wheel that will determine the outcome of races and championships rather than the ability to finance massive engine-development programmes. That, at least, is the theory: but when did theory and practice ever match up in any sport, let alone one so volatile as Formula One? In many people's view, the 1988 season will see a struggle for dominance between McLaren and Lotus, with World Champion Nelson Piquet leading the way for the yellow cars while the rest pick up the crumbs from those rich men's tables . . .

The difficulty of the decision they all faced is clearly shown in the delays in announcing the plans for the Benetton team in 1988. They had a reasonable 1987 with the Ford 1.5-litre turbo engine, scoring points in ten of the sixteen rounds of the World Championship and reaching as high as third place in Austria and Australia. Towards the season's end, if much of the glory was captured by Ferrari's Gerhard Berger, it should be remembered that Thierry Boutsen's Benetton often ran with or ahead of the Austrian in races where niggling mechanical failures cost him dear. So what were Benetton to do: stick with something tried and tested, or go down the atmospheric route with an eye on the 1989 season and equal chances for all? Over to Benetton team manager Peter Collins:

'We simply felt it was the best option for Benetton Formula in 1988, taking into account what Ford could make available to us. We thought the atmospheric engine would be reliable, quite powerful and would give us none of the fuel-consumption worries that will trouble the teams still running with turbo power. After all, producing power is not the problem, but making sure you can run to the full limits of that power right through to the end of the race . . . And we felt the new atmospheric engine was the best way to go among those on offer to us.'

To label the engine 'new' is perhaps slightly misleading, as by the company's own admission the 3.5-litre Ford DFR V8 engine is a refinement of the celebrated Ford Cosworth 3-litre DFV that claimed no fewer than 155 World Championship GP wins in a sixteen-year span from mid-1967. That legendary unit itself spawned the 3.5-litre engine with which Ken Tyrrell decided to attack the 1987 season, hoping perhaps to steal a march on the field as atmospheric days loomed again – and everyone knows the triumphs Ken enjoyed with Cosworth engines in the back of Matras or his own cars.

Tyrrell, in fact, had the glint of battle in his eye again as the 1988 season approached, and a refreshing sight it was. And who could blame Britain's most experienced team manager? After some time in the doldrums with underpowered cars and limited resources, Ken's decision to abandon Renault turbos for Ford naturally-aspirated engines in 1987 was partly a pragmatic business coup of the kind which has made him famous. Before Renault made public their decision to follow their own withdrawal from GP racing with a refusal to supply engines to other manufacturers, Ken was covering himself for the year(s) ahead and at the same time returning to what he liked best. A press conference in Ford's stronghold, Detroit, in the early winter of 1986–7 revealed that Ken had done it again: Ford engines would be his, even if, in the season ahead, they could not hope to compete with the turbo cars on any but the slowest of the street circuits. 'But', reasoned Ken, 'I had two goals in mind for that year: to win the Jim Clark and Colin Chapman cups, and to get in a year of extra atmospheric running before the Formula went that way definitively in 1989.' The first aim was duly achieved when Jonathan Palmer, in a season that did no harm at all to his reputation, claimed the Jim Clark Cup ahead of Tyrrell stablemate Philippe Streiff, and the Tyrrell cars won the atmospheric constructors' division by the proverbial circuit length. What of the second objective? Well, to talk to Ken Tyrrell these days is to address a man with the whiff of grapeshot in his nostrils and an unquenched ambition to be back at the top of GP racing . . .

But the competition among the atmospheric runners of 1988 is going to be pretty keen. First of all, Tyrrell must contend with that new Ford engine to which Benetton have exclusive rights. 'We expect it to generate something around 600 brake horsepower,' opines Peter Collins, 'while the turbo cars are putting out 630 to 650, or at the very upper end maybe 670. That's a dramatic reduction in the difference we saw in 1987, for a start.' In time-honoured fashion, the new Ford engine for 1988 will have eight cylinders, each with five valves: three inlet and two exhaust. The

Left *Palmer's Tyrrell heads Streiff's as was often the case in '87*

Right *Same name, new power for Benetton: Ford naturally-aspirated units in '88*

Ford Motor Company believes the unit's intrinsic qualities will be enhanced by changes in the regulations in the coming season. For one thing, the atmospheric-engined cars will not be subject to any fuel limitation; for another, they will enjoy a weight advantage of no less than 40 kilograms over the turbo cars. In an era which has seen designers falling over themselves to save weight on their cars wherever possible, that represents no little saving, giving further hope to those who hope for somewhat closer racing than we were sometimes treated to in 1987.

Given these potential gains, Peter Collins does not view the loss of the Ford turbocharged engine as something to shed too many tears over. 'The turbo decade was a very exciting one, in my opinion, and would have continued to be exciting. But there was so much development potential to the turbo that it would have been very difficult to contain the speeds Grand Prix cars were capable of, let alone curb them. No use moaning about it, you've just got to get on with the job. Of course there are problems: first and foremost, the new engine requires a different chassis, but in some ways that's fairly easy, in others a bit more difficult. All of it is just part of doing the job – you simply have to adapt.

'We don't see the decision to go atmospheric as a short-term sacrifice at all. Who is to say that we will not be pretty competitive from the start of 1988? After all, there are plenty of people having to make changes on the engine front. McLaren, for instance, have to accommodate their new Honda engines, so they need a new car, while Williams have to adapt to Judd atmospheric engines after all their successes with Honda turbos. We expect to give most of them a run for their money.'

Collins has the added luxury of knowing that, should he want to, he can call on another new Ford power unit from the start of 1989. Ford see the 1988 arrangement as 'part of the programme to design and develop a totally new 3.5-litre naturally-aspirated Ford Formula One engine for the 1989 season'. That unit will also be exclusively available to Benetton in a three-year deal with the engine manufacturer, who plan to make the DFR unit available from then on to other Formula One teams – shades of the late sixties, when the Ford Cosworth was born with Lotus and Colin Chapman firmly in mind but was made available, from 1968, to other teams, much to the chagrin of the great Chapman but greatly to the benefit of the sport and its spectators. Collins is keeping his options open. 'We are not necessarily going to change engines again at the end of this one season,' he concludes. 'We intend to wait and see if we feel there is a real need to do so . . .'

Leaving thoughts of power aside (as if anyone in Formula One ever would!), the other huge area of concern in the turbo has been the cost of engines, a point on which we aired Ken Tyrrell's views in our first *BBC Grand Prix* book. Collins is not convinced by those who welcome the return to normally-aspirated engines solely on the grounds that they will bring sanity back to the budget of each GP team. 'I'm not so sure about this,' he adds. 'Atmospheric engines could prove to be fairly high-cost themselves. All right, some of the individual components may not be as expensive; but engine-rebuild costs may well be pushed up because of the revolutions at which we are having to run and the wear placed on those components as a result. One thing I am sure of is that we are not about to see a return to the good old days of normally-aspirated, cost-efficient engines. Things have changed in Formula One as elsewhere, and we just have to accept that and get on with it.' Wouldn't it be nice if everyone adopted such a straightforward approach?

One man for whom life in Formula One has been less than straightforward since the appearance of the first *BBC Grand Prix* book is one of Britain's most popular drivers, a young man whose driving ambition seemed sure to take him to the top of the tree. But for Martin Brundle things have turned rather sour, and in 1988 he will be so far removed from GP racing as to find himself out of Formula One altogether.

The 1986 season was Martin's third with Ken Tyrrell, and everything seemed set fair for young Brundle to make a name for himself: new sponsors, turbo engines . . . But the Renault units proved a major disappointment, leaving Martin and Philippe Streiff midfield runners at best for most of the season, and at the end of the year Martin was negotiating a new contract – from a position of less than invulnerable strength. 'I had been waiting for the second McLaren seat to be offered to me,' recalls the

Left *Martin Brundle's Zakspeed was not always this uncompetitive . . .*

Below *Keep your hat on, Martin: better times to come*

King's Lynn driver, 'but the longer it dragged on the clearer it became that I was not to be Keke Rosberg's successor in that team. Ken had asked me to re-sign already, but I felt I had to wait and see what opportunities came along. Then by the time the plum drive went to someone else, my options were reduced and it was Ken who was saying he didn't know if he could keep me on.'

Net result: a transfer to the small West German Zakspeed team, with whom Martin knew he would have turbo power, and for whom some off-season testing in the winter gave him heart. 'Better to be a midfield turbo runner than at the back with an atmospheric engine' was the Brundle reasoning, but his season turned to ashes as the promised new Zakspeed failed to materialise and Martin either retired or trailed in hopelessly adrift, sometimes soundly beaten by non-turbo cars. To speak to him intermittently throughout 1987 was to chart the process of disillusionment in a formerly self-confident sportsman left wondering whether he would ever get to the front of the grid.

The process reached its climax in Adelaide. Although Martin did not formally announce his 1988 plans until the start of the year, it was clear from conversations there that the Brundle career in Formula One was, temporarily at least, coming to an end. The main reason? Power games, and the inability to win them. Thoroughly fed up with fighting machinery that did not match his talents, Martin decided to accept an offer outside GP racing that would, in his own words, 'let me get used to winning races again'. For Martin the difference between winning and losing in GP racing is very much a question of engines. 'I had a bad year in '87,' he candidly admits. 'Far from going forward, I think my career actually went backwards – and that's not a direction favoured by most racing drivers! There were a number of problems at Zakspeed, but the crucial one was the unreliability of engines. It's fair to say, I suppose, that this is the major reason for failure to finish races nowadays: the materials used on the car and the ancillary components are now so well made and durable that the engine is easily the most stressed part of a Grand Prix car.'

Martin makes no secret of the fact that engines and their performance were a major factor in the decision-making process that has taken him, temporarily at least, out of GP grids altogether. 'With the changes in regulations for 1988, we just don't know what the performance of the turbos in relation to atmospheric engines is going to be. No one at this stage could honestly stand up and say, "This or that is going to happen" – not that they ever could in Formula One. But my own gut feeling is that by mid-season the winning will be done by atmospheric engines. Bearing in mind the drop of 45 litres in fuel available to the turbo runners – and nearly one quarter of your allowance is a hell of a lot to have to save – I expect to see the atmospheric-engined cars a lot further up than they were last year. If I made a mistake in 1987, in fact, it was in underestimating how quick the non-turbo runners would be. They were always at close quarters with the midfield turbo cars, whereas in 1988 I expect to see them snapping at the heels of the front-running turbo brigade. Having said that,' he adds, 'the Honda V6 turbo will still be the one to beat this season.'

For those who take an interest in Martin's career, it may be interesting to glance sideways at his plans for the immediate future. 'As in 1986–7,' he explains, 'my options for the 1988 season were relatively few in number. A similar situation arose when Nelson Piquet left Williams and I waited for a chance of that drive until Frank Williams made Riccardo Patrese the number two to Nigel Mansell. Being able to call myself "a Grand Prix driver" just wasn't enough any more after four seasons in the sport: there are, in my view, only five teams capable of winning Grands Prix, and maybe three or four that can do so regularly, and they weren't available to me.

'I wanted to be part of a properly-financed, properly-structured team, one that had real wind-tunnel budgets and so on, and unfortunately that was only possible outside Formula One. So I shall be racing for Tom Walkinshaw's Jaguar sports car team in 1988, in North America and throughout Europe. It's well-charted territory for me – I've driven for Tom, mostly in saloons, since 1979. I was in fact the lead driver for Jaguar when they returned to sports-car racing in 1985, but my Tyrrell teammate Stefan Bellof was killed in a Porsche early in the season and Ken Tyrrell understandably asked me to stop that kind of racing.

'In fact people sometimes think of me as quite an experienced sports-car driver, but I've only competed in four sprint races and one Le Mans 24-Hour classic. I'm just back from the States [this is in January 1988], and I believe the competition over there is going to be a lot tougher than some people expect. I'll be doing a lot of racing, maybe with a couple of Grands Prix thrown in for good measure. Out of twenty-five starts or thereabouts, I expect my chances of winning ten or a dozen races to be pretty strong.' After ten retirements in the sixteen-race 1987 GP season, that kind of confidence-booster is exactly what the twenty-eight-year-old Brundle requires before coming back to show the Formula One world what he can really achieve. To press his point he won the Daytona 24-Hours in his Jaguar.

Speaking of Williams, as Martin did, what are the Didcot team's prospects for 1988? World Champion Constructors for the last two seasons, Frank Williams' men face a major change in the coming season, and perhaps a fall from grace after losing those Honda engines we discussed

Top *Seat of power in 1988: the Judd workshop*

Bottom *Patrick Head* (pointing) *discusses the new engine with its builder, John Judd*

earlier. After all, when you have won eighteen races over the last two seasons and been used to life at the sharp end, switching back to 3.5-litre atmospheric engines is no small step.

For 1988, Williams will be one of three teams supplied by a name little known until now to all outside the mainstream of racing. The power units will come from Engine Developments, the Rugby concern run by Englishman John Judd, who has bitten off a man-sized chunk for his entry into the arena of Formula One. Not only will Judd supply engines to Williams, but also to the March and Ligier teams. Rarely has a new entrant into the sport arrived with such a load to carry, but the task of producing some fifty engines for the season leaves the small but go-ahead concern undaunted.

Where Williams are concerned, this is a reunion rather than a new partnership, for one of Judd's earliest involvements with Formula One was with the Didcot team, helping develop the Ford Cosworth engine at the start of this decade. Patrick Head, the Williams designer, knows the pitfalls that lie ahead. 'Switching from the Honda turbo engine to the normally-aspirated Judd V8 was obviously a difficult move. We had enjoyed two-and-a-half good years with Honda, and we had built up a strong working relationship with the Honda engineers. In line with a change in the Formula One engine regulations, however, we decided to work with John Judd and the 3.5-litre V8 engine he had been developing over the past eighteen months.'

So far, so simple – but Head, in his typically matter-of-fact way, now goes straight to the heart of the matter: 'The Judd engine is lighter and more compact than the Cosworth DFZ – perhaps one should add here that the Cosworth is now in its twenty-first year! – and, in our early experience, has combined reliability with good power through the rev range. There is a lot more to come in terms of performance but the real question is how this engine will compare with 1.5-litre turbo engines limited to 2.5-bar boost-pressure and 150 litres of fuel.

'If the turbo and non-turbo engines are closely matched – and we won't really know the answer to that question until the season begins – it could well be the fuel limitation that most influences the equivalence. It is likely that the turbo engines will in themselves be more powerful; fuel consumption worries and, to a lesser extent, inferior throttle response and greater overall weight will possibly be their less attractive features.'

What Patrick Head refers to diplomatically as 'less attractive' is precisely what makes the 1988 prospects so appealing to the man with the heavy responsibility of replacing the power that has made Williams the kings of the Formula One castle for the last two seasons. So it is time to get answers, as it were, straight from the horse's mouth . . .

Above *New colours for 1988: Piquet emerges from the Lotus motor-home in early season testing*

Right *Man of the moment: John Judd*

For John Judd himself, the answer to our first question may seem fairly obvious, but he follows it with a more objective look at the sport's well-being. 'Is the ending of turbochargers a good thing?' we asked discreetly. 'Well, yes,' came the answer, 'because it lets us back in! Seriously, I think it probably is a good thing on balance, because it will make teams more competitive – it will reduce the gap between the haves and have-nots. The gap in performance between us and the turbo cars will depend on where we are racing, but the only place where they will annihilate us is Mexico with its peculiar atmospheric characteristics. They will outqualify us, because there the fuel limitation does not come into play, but they will find themselves at a disadvantage at circuits like Monaco and Detroit. Then again, they should be faster on tracks like Silverstone, but fuel problems may dog them, and I don't think they themselves will be able to forecast until everyone has done a lot more testing.'

What of the past relationship with Williams? Does this mean Frank's team will enjoy some kind of preferential treatment in the Judd scheme of things? 'Not at all' is the swift retort. 'All the work will be shared equally, and we shall be doing our utmost for all concerned.' This includes engine rebuilds: with the actual building taking up to 200 man-hours per unit, rebuilds will demand something in the region of 80–100 man-hours. placing considerable strain – 'Too much!' jokes Judd – on the resources of Engine Developments. 'I expect Williams to be using about seventy-five engines in the course of the year,' he continues. 'Not that this means they will put seventy-five new units into Williams chassis, of course, but on some seventy-five occasions they will be putting a fresh or refreshed

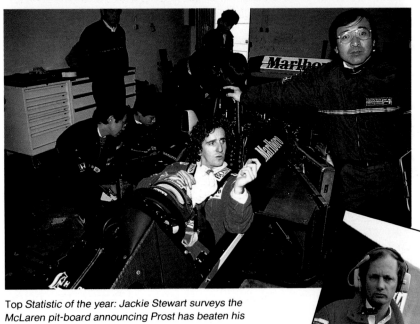

Top *Statistic of the year: Jackie Stewart surveys the McLaren pit-board announcing Prost has beaten his all-time record of 27 wins*

Bottom *A bemused Honda engineer with Prost in the new McLaren–Honda*

Inset *Top man at McLaren: Ron Dennis*

engine in. As for their chances in the World Championship, I see no reason to believe from the outset that they cannot make it three in a row. Look back on 1987's results, and as often as not, outside the first two or three finishers, it's a case of the walking wounded being left. It all depends on the balance they can achieve between speed and reliability.' Anyone at all familiar with the aims of Formula One designers, managers and drivers over the years will know the perennial validity of that particular equation . . .

So much, then, for the arrival of a new face, whose impact on the scene we await eagerly. But as we have seen, most observers feel there will still be hard work ahead for anyone hoping to steal a march on the principal turbo runners. There are three of these. Ferrari's back-to-back victories at Suzuka and Adelaide in late 1987 were welcome news indeed for all who believe that seeing those red cars at the front of the grid is a sign of health in Formula One generally. With Berger and Alboreto in the cockpit, a new John Barnard car ready to roll and the good times back at Maranello, the other two main turbo teams have everything to prove.

Lotus have already pulled off one major coup: losing the gifted Ayrton Senna to McLaren, they promptly replaced him with his fellow-Brazilian Nelson Piquet. Now Nelson, you will recall, just happened to take his third World Championship in 1987, thereby stealing the coveted number one away from the Williams team he was leaving and taking it with him to decorate the front of the blue-and-yellow Lotus. Piquet may take time to settle in at Lotus, though, and who knows what his attitude will be after what he called his hardest-working season ever?

That leaves just one name, and one that used to be the most feared in the GP sphere: McLaren. World Champions in 1984 and 1985, they also gave Niki Lauda and Alain Prost the material to claim three Drivers' World Championships in 1984/5/6 before Honda power in the back of Patrick Head's cars knocked them off the top. Solution to problem? Go out and get Honda engines, which will be allied in 1988 to the unique driving talents of Alain Prost himself and Ayrton Senna. Can the Woking team put everything around the new power unit in time for the start of 1988, we wondered, or would it take time for the new mix to come together? As usual, some very clear answers were forthcoming from Ron Dennis. 'We have been testing considerably since the start of the year,' he said, 'and as we speak Alain [Prost] is testing again for a week out in Japan. In addition to this, we have planned a huge testing programme alongside our racing schedule, and so far the data we have gathered are very, very positive. All of the testing [this again was at the end of January] has been done with the new engine in the 1987 chassis, but the new car is also progressing well and we expect to be ready in time for the Rio test.'

So will McLaren be up there from the off? 'Confidence is a weakness' is one of Mr Dennis's favourite expressions, carefully designed and rationed to temper undue enthusiasm. 'But', he admitted, 'we do expect to be competitive from the start of the season. Ayrton Senna will do his own first testing at Rio, and after that we have some twenty-five sessions planned, so our drivers will both have their work clearly mapped out . . .'

Perhaps the last word on all this should be left to the man who, to all intents and purposes, has benefited most from the move back towards atmospheric engines. Britain's Dr Jonathan Palmer passed Martin Brundle going in the opposite direction at the start of the 1987 season. Not that they were on the track at the time, but only in the sense that as Martin left Tyrrell to try his luck with Zakspeed, Jonathan was ending his spell with the West German team to take over the Brundle seat in Ken's team. The net result for Martin we have seen, but the Palmer story is quite different.

Bringing his usual analytical coolness to bear on the task of getting the

Was it simpler then? Stirling Moss looks at the innards . . .

most out of Tyrrell's Ford engine, Palmer did so to such effect that well before the end of the season Ken was World Champion in the atmospheric division and Palmer himself a Formula One World Champion in his own right. For 1988, he too has his sights set higher still. 'If you ask me what I think the gap will be between turbo and non-turbo cars this season,' he says, 'perhaps I can answer that by saying I intend to go out and try to win the World Championship – I don't expect to be second best throughout. The new regulations are very good for Formula One, from the competitors' point of view and especially for spectators, which is the most important thing. Racing will be a lot closer, and we shan't see the Noah's Ark situation any more – cars coming in two by two!

'There will be a concertina effect on grids and races, which means that a good driver in a mediocre car, say, will be able to put up a much better relative showing. Similarly, a midfield team having a good weekend will now find themselves in with a chance of winning. Not having a fuel limit [which will be the case for everyone in 1989] will also be a good thing: we won't see drivers having to back off because of question marks over how much they have left. Mind you, there has been that element of doubt in recent years: race positions have often changed dramatically in the last few laps, and that's one variable that will no longer apply. Anyway, racing has always operated in a regulations envelope, which has always changed; this is just one more variation.'

It should be plain from all this that 1988 approached with the horizons still not clearly visible. Power games would again be the order of the day, but regulation changes meant that raw power would be balanced by increased stringency on weight and fuel, and there were not a few who felt the atmospheric route was already the one to follow. Whatever the whys and wherefores of this debate at the sport's centre, one thing must be hoped for: that advantages in sheer output and performance, for too long the province only of the richest members of the Formula One club, should not for much longer stand in the way of the natural aspirations of the sport's finest driving talents.

6 TYRED AND EMOTIONAL

If motor-racing is renowned for the spectacular and memorable images it throws up, none is more firmly engraved in the minds of British followers than that of Nigel Mansell's exit from the 1986 Australian GP. The Englishman, driving for Williams, needed to finish no higher than third to take the Drivers' World Championship, the first Briton to do so since James Hunt a decade before. As is now part of sporting folklore, Mansell was not destined to wear the crown: as he cruised along in third place with nineteen laps to go, a sudden tyre failure saw his afternoon transformed in an instant from the pursuit of glory to the preservation of his very life. Deprived of balance and traction at something like 200 mph, he needed all the skill honed in long years behind a wheel to control the dancing, bucking Williams and come to a bitterly frustrated halt in one of the Adelaide circuit's exit roads.

In the minutes, hours and months after that decisive race, the photographic record of Mansell's terrifying few seconds would point up perhaps the most significant area in the make-up of a racing car: its tyres. There are, after all, only four tiny points of contact between this aerodynamic missile and terra firma, and those are stretched to the limit by the tolerances within which the modern GP car works. How would you like to be cornering at 150 mph or so with only a few square centimetres of rubber between you and oblivion?

This is the responsibility adopted by the suppliers of tyres to the Formula One teams, and in the Adelaide instance it was a Goodyear tyre that failed. What followed was an example of refreshing honesty on that company's part as, in the light of what had happened to Mansell, they advised the Williams team to call Mansell's team-mate, Nelson Piquet, in for a tyre change. The respect the drivers have for the men who make their machinery is underlined by Piquet's ready acceptance of the decision,

Opposite *Racing service: one of the Goodyear trucks*

Inset *The moment that cost Mansell the 1986 title*

even though it most probably cost him the World Championship to which he too was an aspirant.

For Goodyear, now the exclusive suppliers of tyres to GP racing, the incident prompted a comprehensive reappraisal of their activities, and one which produced some interesting opinions on the state of Formula One. For instance, partly in self-defence the company – based in Akron, Ohio – was obliged to air its views on current practice amongst racing teams. As a spokesman explains, 'Tyre failure and other Formula One problems had been masked by pit stops. Who knows? The tyre failure or something similar might have happened earlier in the season if drivers had been in the habit of going full distance without a stop for fresh tyres. We might draw a parallel here with the famous wheel-nut incident that robbed Nigel Mansell of victory in Hungary in 1987.

'In Goodyear's defence, for instance, we might ask: what is the difference between Mansell's tyre failure – and reluctantly we must call it that – and the breaking of a drive-shaft in Austria or a turbo somewhere else? It is, after all, just another component failure in a sport where these occur by the minute, and a look at the record books would probably show that tyre failures are proportionally far fewer than those of any other of the components on a Grand Prix car.

'But we are penalised because a tyre is one of the most visible parts of these complex machines, our name is all round its circumference, and when a tyre goes it has such visual, spectacular impact. Hence the publicity for Adelaide '86, and the rather exaggerated – in our view – impression left in the public mind by what happened to one of England's sporting heroes. In the last analysis, however, it is fair to say that we did learn lessons from Adelaide '86 – but then the company position is that the day we stop learning is the day we may as well quit Formula One definitively.'

Before contemplating such a radical departure, it may be useful to look back briefly at the history of tyre companies in Formula One. Many have come, several have gone, and a few have made a significant contribution to the advancement of tyre technology in what is supposed, after all, to be the ultimate proving ground. In the earliest days of the World Championship, and into the sixties, it was a virtual Dunlop monopoly. For the English company that happy state of affairs lasted only until the arrival of Firestone in 1964 and the entry of Goodyear on the scene a season later.

With the coming of the American giant, things were about to change dramatically; while a primitive version of 'tyre wars' may have gone on two decades ago, it was not until the late seventies that real conflict began. One reason was the appearance of the other giant corporation in tyre production. Michelin, based in Clermont-Ferrand with all its historical associations with motor-racing, were determined to take Goodyear

Above *High, not so wide and not very handsome: how tyres used to be*

Right *Look, three wheels: Yannick Dalmas in a lame Lola at Suzuka in 1987*

Tyres have to contend with features like Spa's La Source hairpin, seen here with Prost's McLaren. Inset Stewart shows off the difference between slick and wet tyres

on. They supplied tyres to Renault – themselves just launching their ill-fated Formula One onslaught – and Ferrari in 1977, but 1978 was to be their first full season. One year later they were World Champions with Scheckter's Ferrari, a feat they repeated with Ferrari and Brabham in 1983 and 1984 before abruptly ending their involvement with GP racing.

The reasons for this relatively short stay are straightforward enough, and they centre around one of the technical advances we referred to: the radial tyre. For a very long time indeed – and for some years as a rearguard strategy of Goodyear's – cross-ply tyres held sway in Formula One as elsewhere. Taller and thinner than the tyres we recognise today, cross-plies were built up in layers, sometimes four deep, of man-made textiles moulded into rubber and topped off with a rubber compound that might be one-fifth of an inch thick, and grew in subsequent seasons to two or three times that depth. The final compound itself would be the fruit of chemical labours more akin to Macbeth's lady friends than the high-tech input now so familiar in motor-racing, but all that hubble, bubble, toil and trouble paid dividends until Michelin came along.

For when they did, it was to take into new areas of experience a tyre they had introduced on road-going cars as early as 1946: the radial, known in its early days as the Michelin X. As distinct from the cross-ply, the radial laid its layers (or 'ply') at a supposed ninety degrees to the direction of travel, though experts later disputed the angle. The strength of the new construction simultaneously enhanced the flexibility of tyre sidewalls, one of the weaknesses inherent in cross-ply construction that had bedevilled designers of ever-faster cars. Moreover, radial-ply tyres could run at inherently cooler temperatures, this in turn permitting the use of ever-softer, stickier compounds – all this in search of that little extra bit of grip and stability to earn the vital hundredth of a second over the next man on the race grid. Tyre performance has a knock-on effect, too, on the suspension of the car, an area which itself has become of paramount importance in recent months as both Lotus and Williams have tried their own variants of a radical, computer-controlled hydro-pneumatic suspension labelled 'active ride' and touted as the next major contribution of GP racing to car technology as a whole.

That unending search for grip also led to the introduction – this time by Goodyear themselves – of so-called 'slick' tyres as far back as 1971. These are, quite simply, enormous tyres with the tread channels taken away so that a greater area of rubber is in contact with the track surface at any one time, with concomitant improvement in tyre temperature and road-holding ability. Brought in at Kyalami seventeen years ago, these slick tyres are in dramatic contrast to 'wets', which are nothing to do with modern British politics but more conventional tyres with deep channels

Groovy: Boutsen's Benetton in the wet at Spa

to direct rainwater away both from the tyre itself and from the small area of track being covered at any one moment. The 'wets' are made of ultra-soft compounds that will allow the generation of heat, and therefore grip, despite the presence of large amounts of water and its cooling effect.

Tyres, in fact, played their own crucial part in the creation of a state of affairs recently condemned by many onlookers at GP racing: the special madness known as qualifying. In 1981 the regulations stipulated that each car might enjoy only two sets of special, ultra-soft qualifying tyres per one-hour session of timed practice. This made possible those kami-kaze laps – which, to be fair, were often more thrilling in themselves than much of the racing – in which drivers risked all to extract the maximum performance from tyres that would 'go off' with astonishing rapidity. Frustrations, built up when mechanical failure, say, or the oft-lamented 'traffic' would lay waste to a driver's flying lap, have been the cause of more than one hair-raising incident in recent seasons. There are those who blame the qualifying-tyre situation for the death of the great Gilles Villeneuve in practice for the 1982 Belgian GP at Zolder, and there can be no doubt that the pressure to do away with qualifying in that form was growing. But more of that anon . . .

Just as France, then, led the way in car building and in competition at the beginnings of it all in the late nineteenth century, so Michelin – who themselves patented the pneumatic tyre a hundred years ago – were

Michelin heyday: Lauda and Prost in dominant form in the 1984 McLarens

using Formula One as, in the company's own words, 'an exacting test bed' for tyre technology. Racing, as they reasoned, created specially-controlled conditions in which all aspects of tyre performance – pressures, temperatures, wear rates – were scrupulously monitored in practice and in the races themselves. Success in GP racing meant prestige for the competitor and the tyre company that contributed to his triumphs. So why withdraw, as Michelin did, when everything in the French back garden seemed so rosy?

A fairly terse bulletin issued on 24 September 1984 by racing director Pierre Dupasquier explains: 'When we entered Formula One our primary objective was to prove the capabilities of our radial-tyre technology. Since that time we have won more F1 races than all of our competitors combined. We have clinched three World Championships. We also have learned a lot.' For them, the competition tyre was closely linked to the technology of production-car tyres and racing was the ultimate test of road-holding quality. As Dupasquier slyly added, 'We have seen with great interest the competition finally shifting from the bias-ply tyre to the radial.' To add weight to his statements, Michelin in that final year of 1984 recorded fourteen wins in the sixteen-race season, taking pole position thirteen times and setting fifteen fastest laps, though much of the credit must also go, of course, to the superb chassis–engine package of the McLaren and the driving skills of Messrs Prost and Lauda. Dominant in motor sport from its inception until 1910, Michelin had endured a fifty-year absence before coming back to re-prove the superiority of their technology.

They are not the only ones to have come and gone from Formula One, however. Firestone pulled out in 1974, and today's kings Goodyear themselves withdrew for a much briefer period before returning to become the dominant force they are today. The reason? In late 1980, as spokesman Barry Griffin recalls, the political wranglings that threatened to split Formula One asunder (see Chapter 2) were so bad for the image of GP racing and all involved that Goodyear could no longer justify their presence. 'The image was no longer that of a dynamic, thriving sports and business scene; it had become tarnished and we were in danger of being tarred with the same brush. So it was a good time to get out for six months, as we eventually did, and in that time Formula One was able to get its act together and become attractive once more.' As an amusing digression, it should be recalled that this opened the door for such companies as Avon to come in and, in Doug Nye's graphic phrase, 'keep the cannon-fodder teams mobile'!

Griffin is candid enough to admit that the six-month separation gave pause for thought on both sides, and for assessing the lessons learned from it. 'That temporary absence', he reflects, 'enabled us at Goodyear to measure the value of Formula One to us. It was not just a question of what we could be seen to be doing for the sport, but what motor-racing meant to Goodyear. We already knew, of course, but that period underlined the fact that perhaps this Grand Prix racing was not such a bad thing after all . . . Whatever form of words you care to choose, it is fair to say that we were very pleased to come back.'

Back with a vengeance, you might say, for Goodyear now find themselves sole suppliers of racing rubber to all the teams taking part in Formula One. This happy state of affairs for the Ohio company comes about as a result of what Tony Howard, in his eminently readable book on Formula One, *Countdown to a Grand Prix*, referred to as 'Tyre Wars'. The allusion to a famous sci-fi movie is not without justification, both in terms of the high technology now involved in the production of racing rubber, the scale of costs, and the struggle for control of the GP empire. Following the withdrawal of Michelin, that war was fought between two companies: Goodyear and Pirelli.

Look at any list of entrants for a GP as recently as the 1986 season, when the first *BBC Grand Prix* book came out, and you will see after each car the letter G or P in brackets. This is to indicate which company is supplying tyres to the team involved, but the insignificance of the letter bears no relation to the crucial part played by the tyres in the performance of

Name of the game: Goodyear looms large

the cars themselves. Modern developments have pushed the capability of GP cars to such extremes that the tyre-makers have struggled to keep pace. A turbo-powered racer such as those that dominated from 1984 to 1987, for example, would generate some 850 horsepower in race-trim and a fearsome 1100 or more in qualifying set-up. It is this latter situation that Goodyear responded to, in competition with the likes of Pirelli, and which they have subsequently tried to circumvent by the imposition of their own conditions for the supply of tyres.

Griffin again: 'If you asked me what had been the most significant development in the history of Goodyear's Formula One involvement, I would have to say it was the move from cross-ply tyres to radials. Not that we made the move merely in response to other companies' own progress: it was essential to do so because of the developments in engine technology. We began producing radial-ply rain tyres in 1983 and slicks [dry-weather tyres] the following year because we needed the strength of the radial to handle the power of turbo-charged engines. It is impossible, you see, to control the diameter of a cross-ply tyre the way you can a radial; a cross-ply grows with centrifugal force such as is exerted – massively – in the cornering of a Grand Prix racing car, so radials were the only way to go as those forces grew under the pressure of power development. And you must bear in mind that Goodyear cannot make tyres of any size they want: like everything else in the Grand Prix world, tyre dimensions are carefully laid down by FISA, and we have simply had to accept the challenge of producing tyres within those parameters and for the peculiar job they have to do.

'Next season, for example, as we witness the gradual phasing-out of turbocharged engines, we shall not be reducing the tyre size we produce, but we shall be better able to handle the power the latest cars will generate. Putting it another way, it is possible to say that the famous – or do I mean notorious? – Mansell incident might not have occurred under the regulations that will apply from the start of the 1988 season. It is difficult to express the power that turbocharged engines gave to Grand Prix cars – but if I remind you that a Formula One car of that generation is able to spin its wheels in fifth gear, that gives you some idea of what is going on down there!'

As for the sheer scale of effort involved in the production of racing tyres, Griffin is equally matter-of-fact. No tyres emanate from the company's Wolverhampton facility, all of the Formula One production being centred on Akron, Ohio. It can take days, or even weeks, to assemble all the components that go into the making of each tyre: treads have to be extruded, the fabric for the casing has to be impregnated with rubber, and so on. But once all those components are in place it is a matter of minutes to put the tyre itself together.

'I would put it at no more than a few minutes,' says Griffin, 'after which the tyre has to be literally baked, or "cured", as the process is known, for forty-five minutes or so. Formula One consumes something like 30,000 tyres a year, and a fair estimate of the cost is $300 per unit. If shipping and duties are added, we reckon the true cost at about $500, but where the paying teams are concerned the cost to them is around $300. We prefer to call this a service charge, because it might be very damaging to a team's sponsorship prospects if a potential backer heard that Goodyear were actually making them pay for their tyres. Not well-enough fancied to be given the company's products free, eh? Rather than have a team manager go to his sponsor and say he needs another chunk of money to go out and put tyres on his cars, we think the term "service charge" is more appropriate to the relationship we enjoy with the sport.'

That relationship is now in the form of an exclusive arrangement. In the days of ferocious struggles for pole position and front places on the Grand Prix grids, the development of tyres was such that compounds proliferated according to the type of circuit, the speeds likely to be attained, the power output anticipated in lightweight qualifying trim, and the input from each particular driver. Oh yes, the 'feel' of the car is still important to some of them . . .

As Michelin, Pirelli and Goodyear fought out their particular battle in

Look, no wheels: but the specials used to trundle cars in and out of the garage can look worth their weight in gold

these power wars, so costs and burdens grew: there would be sets of tyres with different compounds, either numbered or initialled depending on the company, and ranging, in Goodyear's case, from the very hard 'A' to the ultra-soft 'E' used, more often than not, for qualifying purposes when the cars were scrabbling for every fraction of grip in those frantic hour-long sessions that determine grid positions. Something, some-where, had to give, and at the end of 1986 it was Pirelli, who had simply had enough of the exhausting effort of supplying a number of racing teams with a huge number of tyres once a fortnight in a season stretching from March to November, to say nothing of the innumerable tyre tests at other circuits in between races. This was the opportunity Goodyear needed to impose their will, and after threatening their own withdrawal from the GP scene, they returned at the start of 1987 with a specific offer.

'We asked each team to sign an agreement,' explains Griffin. 'Not a contract in strict terms, but an agreement to use Goodyear tyres exclu-sively. That gave us the protection we sought from a state of affairs in which a team might sign a deal with, say, Pirelli, and that company would make available a variety of tyres or compounds and force us to do the same merely to allow our supplied teams to compete. We would have been obliged to give our leading teams everything we could, while the ones at the other end of the grid found themselves the poor relations. In that case Goodyear, who are in the sport to win for Goodyear and not for any particular team, would have been seen as the villains of the piece. The agreement we reached with the teams at the start of 1987 was done to prevent Goodyear's being vulnerable.

'Being sole supplier is not a bad position to be in – if you believe that you really will be the sole supplier. For us it has worked very well. We supply only three compounds: one is for street circuits (in which, because of its peculiar characteristics, we include the Hungaroring at Budapest that came on the scene two years ago); another is for the high-speed circuits, by which I mean Silverstone, Monza and Austria's Zeltweg; and the last or medium compound is used at the other tracks.

'Being sole supplier has not placed upon Goodyear the burden you might imagine, simply because we are free of the responsibility of providing those qualifying tyres. We decide beforehand what compounds will be offered to the teams at a given circuit, so the number of tyres involved is no greater than under the old regime.

'Each driver – driver, not team – is allowed ten sets of tyres per Grand Prix, with a completely fresh batch for every race we go to – even if the next circuit on the calendar requires exactly the same type of tyre as the one we have just left. This ensures that nobody can bypass the system and gain any kind of unfair advantage, for instance by keeping a set of softer tyres such as would be used for Monaco to use as their qualifying tyres at, say, Silverstone. There are numbers on rear and front tyres in

Rubber galore: McLaren taking few chances

Practice makes pit stops and tyre changes perfect: seven seconds is now the norm

every set for every Grand Prix so that the system can be carefully monitored.

'By and large, it has worked to our satisfaction. No one has actually complained in round terms, although of course there has been the odd quibble. These have come mainly from the non-turbo teams, claiming they require softer compounds than the turbo brigade, but generally speaking I think it fair to say that no team has been penalised by the imposition of a particular type of tyre. Race reports from last year indicate that the non-turbo teams did have trouble getting enough heat into their tyres [i.e. getting them to the temperature at which the tyres perform at their peak] but no other gripes emerged.'

The confident tone of these statements is proof, if any were needed, that Goodyear feel they have made their own significant contribution to the development of Formula One and to the internal stability of the sport in particular. Does the company echo the sentiments expressed by Michelin on the gains and pitfalls encountered in Formula One?

'The first purpose behind our racing programme was to create a worldwide awareness of the Goodyear name as a young, vibrant, exciting company,' says Griffin in the adspeak language so familiar from our Sunday supplements and a million handouts. The second point is perhaps less platitudinous and certainly one to bear in mind. 'Formula One is a super training ground for personnel. There is no time to stand around at a Grand Prix, with team managers, mechanics and often drivers screaming at you: you must be able to work very quickly and respond very quickly to situations that arise or change with dramatic suddenness.' Anyone who has wandered up and down a Formula One pit lane, or watched a lightning-quick tyre change from his armchair, will vouch for that: last season, for example, the top teams were actually getting a car into the pits and changing all four wheels in something under seven seconds, and anything over ten seconds was considered antediluvian. Consider the work that goes into preparing those tyres and getting them on to the pit lane before the car screams in, and you can see the force of Griffin's logic.

As our picture shows, that preparation can include some incongruous sights. If speed plus reliability is the criterion for the racing car and its engine, the watchword for tyres is heat. Hence the bizarre sight, in such sunny places as Rio or Monaco, of drivers and team managers huddling under parasols for shade while the tyres on the waiting cars are being gently cooked in the special wrap-around 'electric blankets' that are now a common sight. This is to cut to the absolute minimum the time lapse before a racing tyre 'comes in', as the drivers call it, i.e. the time it takes the rubber compound to reach its optimum working temperature. Hence the small army of Goodyear personnel who patrol the pit lane with fiendish-looking probes that enable them to take a tyre's temperature and monitor likely wear-rates for the expectant team. Hence, too, the myriad small slips of paper exchanged by Goodyear and team personnel as the relative performance of all four tyres is compared: such data will affect, often crucially, the choice of tyres on a given circuit; if there are several fast right-hand turns, for example, the load and stress on the front left tyre will increase proportionately, and a different compound may be called for than is used at the other three corners. Heat, grip and overall resilience: the magic formula for tyre choices which in recent years have been amongst the most critical decisions for driver or team manager to make.

But to return to Goodyear. A final, frank word from Griffin is that the company quite simply enjoys the advertising spin-off from its exposure through GP racing. This has applied throughout the company's involvement, but is obviously the greater now that Goodyear are sole suppliers. Better to be the star of the show, after all, than share top billing with somebody else. Ask any regular GP journalist about Goodyear and as likely as not he will refer to some of the other, less obvious benefits of their presence, such as a free and endless supply of lap charts, or the excellent hospitality on offer in the Goodyear mobile home. These, however, are mere adjuncts to the business that is Formula One today, and the sport has more than one reason to be grateful for Goodyear's input, in recent years particularly.

Best, perhaps, to leave the last word to a driver, and one whom Goodyear helped to a World Championship in 1987. Jonathan Palmer took the honours in the normally-aspirated division last season and, as always, comes straight to the point: 'Apart from the changes on the engine front

Left *Paradox of GP racing: keep the driver cool and the tyres hot*

Below *Tyre change technique: Piquet, Brabham, Detroit . . .*

Bottom *. . . and Williams in action in France*

Ever wonder where old tyres go when their racing days are over?

that we are now seeing, the constancy of the tyre situation is very good at the moment, though there is a cloud on that horizon with the rumoured return of other manufacturers. There is nothing you can do about that, but in my view it will be, quite simply, to the detriment of competition.' And that, perhaps, is the least emotional statement we shall hear on a subject which has often generated the most intense debate in Formula One in recent years . . .

7 THE BRITISH GRAND PRIX

Despite the date – the 13th – luck was on everybody's side. The sky was blue, the sun shone, spring was in the air. The Grenadier Guards played through their well-rehearsed routine, and old and young alike in the 150,000 crowd were enjoying the heady atmosphere.

How many of them, on that long-ago Saturday, as they waited for the arrival of their beloved King George VI and Queen Elizabeth, realised that they were in at the very birth of what is now the Formula One World Championship? For this was Silverstone on 13 May 1950. Silverstone, which just two years before had been a Northamptonshire airfield, previously used by the RAF for training Wellington bomber crews.

Now the roar came not from lumbering aeroplanes but from throaty Alfa-Romeos and an eager crowd enjoying post-war prosperity. This was the first British Grand Prix in the World Championship – indeed the first *ever* Grand Prix in the World Championship. The start, with the front row of *four* Alfas hurling themselves forward towards Woodcote Corner – yes, Woodcote Corner – was the first of 452 Grands Prix to have been contested by the end of 1987 – thirty-eight of them the British GP, the British way of motoring life.

Why Woodcote and not Copse? Because for that first race (and the next) the start-line was just before the bridge after Abbey Curve, with the pits on the infield along the straight into Woodcote.

To Silverstone, then, went the honours of that first race, but to be fair to British racing fans – and to Brooklands – the first-ever *English* Grand Prix was raced over 287 miles of the famous banked Surrey track as far back as 1926. Then Robert Senechal and Louis Wagner shared their Delage to win a Brooklands race *with chicanes* at an average speed of 71.6 mph – not quite the 151.97 mph that Sir John Cobb managed on his way to setting the track speed record on another occasion.

There was just one more year of Grand Prix glory for the Weybridge circuit, in the following year. Again a Delage took the honours, with Robert Benoist at the wheel pushing up the average speed to a pulsating

Royal blessing: the start of the World Championship at Silverstone in 1950

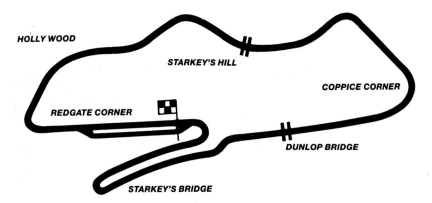

HOLLY WOOD

STARKEY'S HILL

COPPICE CORNER

REDGATE CORNER

DUNLOP BRIDGE

STARKEY'S BRIDGE

DONINGTON PARK

85.6 mph! Then the British scene went into something of a trough, with a seven-year gap before a new circuit appeared in the Midlands. Donington Park boasted four British GPs on the trot – if that is the right word to describe the Alfas of Richard Shuttleworth and Dick Seaman which took the chequered flags in 1935 and 1936. In 1937 and 1938 the Auto Unions took over, with Tazio Nuvolari pushing the Mercedes Benzes of Hermann Lang and Seaman into second and third places over the 250 miles of the Derbyshire track in that last race. Who knows what

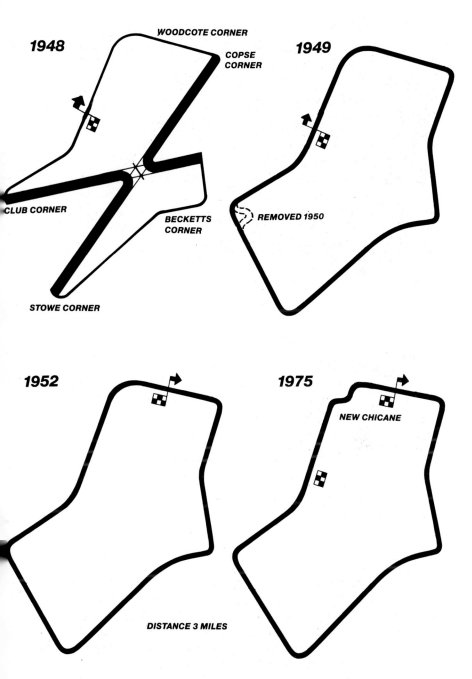

1948

WOODCOTE CORNER

COPSE CORNER

CLUB CORNER

BECKETTS CORNER

STOWE CORNER

1949

REMOVED 1950

1952

DISTANCE 3 MILES

1975

NEW CHICANE

THE CHANGING FACE OF SILVERSTONE

Left *Donington Park, 1937: Mercedes in flight . . .*

Below *. . . and dominating the pit lane*

would have happened in the next decade had those war clouds not gathered across the English Channel?

So to 1948 and what was to be the beginning of it all. As Peter Carrick recalls in his splendid book, *Silverstone – the Story of Britain's Fastest Track*, Brooklands 'had died with the war' and Donington was still requisitioned by the War Office. The Royal Automobile Club, the sport's governing body, did not know where to turn for a replacement for the pre-war tracks, but the British Racing Drivers' Club and its President, Lord Howe, had already arranged with the Air Ministry a one-year lease (with an option of extension) of an aerodrome near Towcester for the running of motor-racing. Silverstone was born.

An October sun picked out the browning greens of autumn as Lord Howe dropped the Union Jack to start the twenty-five-car race. Baron Emmanuel de Graffenried gunned his Maserati into the first corner – and out; Leslie Johnson's half-shaft flew off and ripped into the fuel tank of his ERA; Reg Parnell caught a flying stone in the face; Geoff Ansell crashed his ERA into the barrier at Maggots. Bob Gerard had better luck with his ERA, taking on board oil, water and thirty gallons of fuel in a 45-second pit stop. Straining for a better view, the enormous crowd spilled on to the track for a while, but after 250 miles Italian Luigi Villoresi took that first-ever Silverstone chequered flag in his Maserati, at an average speed of 72.2 mph. A new era in British motor-racing sport had begun.

The 1949 race saw the good Baron make up for his disappointment the previous year by taking the laurels – but he had to drive an extra fifty miles. The race that May took in 300 miles of a different-looking Silverstone, and de Graffenried only took 3 hours 52 minutes 50.2 seconds, to win at an average speed of 77.3 mph.

Why a new circuit after only one year? A look at the1948 track clearly shows that the sharp right-handers at Copse and Stowe meant that cars were hurtling head-on towards each other at combined speeds of nearly 200 mph, with only 'a line of tubs and flags' separating the two infield U-turns. What price a walk-out by today's safety-conscious gladiators faced with such an interesting configuration?

These then were the early days of British Grand Prix racing, the cornerstone on which Stirling Moss, Innes Ireland, Peter Collins, Mike Hawthorn, John Surtees, Jim Clark, Graham Hill, Jackie Stewart, James Hunt, John Watson and Nigel Mansell were to build – much later – their careers. From 1950 to 1987 there have been thirty-eight British Grands Prix – twenty-one at Silverstone, twelve at Brands Hatch and five at Aintree. If you include the two Grands Prix of Europe held at Brands in 1983 and 1985, there has been a grand total of forty FIA-recognised races in the British Isles – more than any other country in the world.

Each of the circuits has its peculiarities, its fans and its detractors. The rivalry between the tracks themselves is intense: Brands was incensed when Silverstone won a deal for five consecutive British GPs from 1987, while Donington's Tom Wheatcroft, the Leicester builder turned million-aire racetrack owner, is 'furious' that he hasn't been allowed to run a car GP (although he was mollified a little by being awarded the British Motor Cycle GP in 1987, 1988 and 1989). After all, he points out, didn't Donington do enough in the thirties to put the East Midlands circuit on the map?

The sad truth is that, despite the money that Wheatcroft has poured into his beloved track since he bought it in 1971, the circuit, with its sausage-like appendage (see diagram) added to give it Grand Prix credence, is considered by some to be too narrow and to have facilities – pits, commentary boxes, grandstands, paddock and so on – well below acceptable worldwide racing standards. Indeed FOCA's Bernie Ecclestone even publicly criticised Silverstone's scaffolding grandstands and hot-dog stalls at the 1987 race. So what price Donington in comparison, where – for the record – the minimum width of the track is 35 ft compared with Silverstone's 46 ft?

Before looking at the two current tracks, however, let us consider the only other home circuit to host a World Championship Formula One race – Aintree. The Liverpool 'course', so famous for so long for four-legged horsepower, hosted the British GP in 1955, 1957, 1959, 1961

Motor racing returns after the war: the 250-mile International Trophy at Silverstone with Bob Gerard (16, back right) prominent in the ERA, 1948

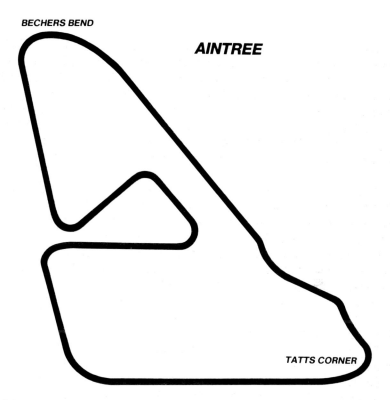

BECHERS BEND

AINTREE

TATTS CORNER

and 1962. Three miles long and built to follow a great part of the Grand National course, when the circuit was opened in 1954 the races were run anti-clockwise. However, by the time a youthful Stirling Moss took pole position in his Mercedes for the 1955 GP, in a time of 2m. 00.4s., he and the rest of the grid were pointing in the more conventional clockwise direction.

With such familiar-sounding track names as Valentine's 'Way' and Becher's 'Bend' to negotiate ninety times, the twenty-five-year-old Moss brought the packed and patriotic grandstand to its feet as he ended the dominance of foreign winners of the British race, pipping the great Juan-Manuel Fangio to the post and, in those days of cars with no weight limits and running at 750cc with a compressor or 2500cc without, recording the fastest lap at 90.2 mph. Fangio was not to be denied his glory that year, though: he went on to win the World Drivers' Championship (as he had done in 1951 and 1954 and would do again in 1956 and 1957). No one else has won the title five times (or even four times) – and neither are they likely to in today's fickle multi-million-dollar world of jumpy sponsors and changing engine manufacturers.

Two years later Stirling had swapped drives – to a Vanwall – but it didn't make any difference. Pole position, fastest lap and the chequered flag all belonged to him over Aintree's 270 miles. It was, though, the end of Moss's love affair with the circuit: he was never to win another British GP. In his sixty-six races over ten years, with sixteen wins, one of Britain's most respected drivers was to finish second in the drivers' championship no fewer than four times and third three times. Surely the unluckiest British driver of them all – including Nigel Mansell!

If a Pom could not win his home GP, the next best thing was an Aussie – and Jack Brabham duly obliged in 1959, driving his Cooper Climax over a shortened circuit of 225 miles. In second place – who else but Stirling Moss. All the more galling for him that Brabham went on to win the title that year and again in 1960. Back at Aintree in 1961 the German Wolfgang von Trips was to win his second – and last – GP. His Ferrari was followed home by his American team-mates Phil Hill (who went on to be World Champion) and Richie Ginther. Two races later – at Monza, of all places – von Trips crashed into the crowd, killing himself and thirteen spectators.

Aintree claimed the British GP again the following year but the writing was already on the track for the Liverpool circuit, even as a new star was being born. He was Scotland's Jim Clark, his car was a Lotus, and he made sure of his victory, the second of his career, by comfortably leaving fellow Brit John Surtees in a Ferrari nearly half a minute in his wake.

But back to Silverstone. 'Royal' Silverstone in 1950 had seen yet another change to the circuit, albeit minute. The Club Corner S-bends were replaced by a more gentle right-hander and the circuit length had shrunk by a tenth of a mile, to 2.9 miles. The good doctor, Giuseppe Farina, led the Alfa-Romeo invasion, and indeed, as Doug Nye says in his 1977 book, *The British Grand Prix*, the outcome of the race was assured as soon as the big Alfa trucks bumped into the paddock. Their Majesties witnessed a 1–2–3 for the Italian marque – but at least Britain's Reg Parnell was a popular third in his privately entered Alfa. Not a great race, but a great landmark in the history of the British Grand Prix. Farina went on to become the first World Champion.

Those first six British World Championship races at Silverstone, 1950–4 and 1956, put the Northamptonshire track – and the British Isles – firmly on the world motor-racing map. But despite some sterling performances by the popular Argentinian Froilan Gonzalez in 1951 and 1954 (his only victories, incidentally), by Italian Alberto Ascari back to

Opposite *Coolest man around: five-time World Champion Juan-Manuel Fangio and his wife at Silverstone in 1954.* Inset left *Fangio in action at Aintree, 1955;* right *Same venue, Hawthorn in full flow, 1959*

Top *The first World Champion: Giuseppe Farina at Silverstone in the inaugural year, 1950*
Bottom *British favourites Stuart Lewis-Evans (left), Stirling Moss and Mike Hawthorn at
Silverstone in 1958: Peter Collins won, Hawthorn was second, Lewis-Evans fourth and
Moss started from pole*

back in 1952 (the year which saw the start/finish area moved to the straight between Woodcote and Copse, with new pits and grandstands) and 1953 – in both years on his way to the world title, and inevitably by fellow Argentinian Fangio in 1956 on the way to the fourth of his five world titles, the hugely partisan Silverstone fans were denied the one thing they wanted most – a British winner (Moss had won at Aintree in 1955 and 1957). Then at Silverstone in 1958 it all changed.

Doug Nye again: 'The new season saw fundamental changes to the character of Formula One Grand Prix racing which gave the emergent British "special builders" the chance they needed to get on terms with the new established constructors, such as Vanwall and Ferrari. Financial difficulties had seen the demise of Maserati as a serious works team at the end of 1957 and the Commission Sportive Internationale had bowed to oil company pressures by banning alcohol-based fuels and stipulating 130-octane "Avgas" petrol in its place.' Race distances were also relaxed, organisers being allowed to cut back from 500 km (approximately 310.5 miles) to 300 km (approximately 186.5 miles) if they wished, and from three hours' to two hours' duration.

As it happened, a Ferrari was to win that 1958 race, but the big difference – apart from a race of only 219.5 miles – was that at the wheel of the Ferrari was Britain's Peter Collins. Only on the second row of the grid, behind Moss (pole), Schell, Salvadori and Hawthorn, and sandwiched between Allison and Lewis-Evans, the twenty-seven-year-old Collins took a flyer and surged past Moss's Vanwall to take the lead. Other drivers came and went, including France's Jean Behra who, after hitting one of Silverstone's famous hares, suffered the ultimate indignity of a tyre punctured by one of the poor creature's bones! Collins came home to win, breaking the 100 mph average lap-speed barrier, and towing three fellow countrymen – Hawthorn, Salvadori and Lewis-Evans – behind him to take the first four places for Britain.

The celebrations had barely stopped when, two weeks later at the German GP at Nürburgring, Peter Collins was killed. To complete a black year for motor-racing, Lewis-Evans suffered fatal burns in the Moroccan GP, the last of the season, at Casablanca; and Mike Hawthorn, who had gone on to pip Stirling Moss by just one point to become the first British World Champion, was also killed – in a road accident on the Guildford bypass.

Two more popular Silverstone winners beckoned now. As a new decade of motor-racing began in 1960, so did that Golden Era of British drivers. There was a real Commonwealth feel to the front row of that seventy-seven-lap race, with Aussie Jack Brabham in his Cooper Climax in pole, Britain's Graham Hill in the BRM next, and the second Cooper, of

Top *Peter Collins in the Ferrari, Silverstone 1958. He was killed just two weeks later*

Bottom *First British World Champion Mike Hawthorn*

Inset *Never quite in the top flight: Roy Salvadori at Brands Hatch in 1959*

Kiwi Bruce McLaren, third. The day was also to provide a great spectacle and, as Graham Hill himself reflected, 'what was probably one of my best races – but I made a real monkey's of it at the start'. He did, too – stalling on the line and, for his pains, getting a 'push start' from Tony Brooks. Not to worry. Hill worked his way through the field, caught and passed Brabham, the leader, and with only five laps to go spun off passing backmarkers. Jack took the flag and no one in the crowd objected after a thrilling race.

By the time the Formula One circus was to pitch its tent again at Silverstone – three years later in 1963 – the public was already into a new British motor-racing phenomenon – the one and only Jim Clark. Clark, remember, had clinched the British GP the previous year at Aintree, and had followed this with two more wins, in Belgium and America. But at the end of the season the World Champion was one of the most popular British drivers ever to win the title. Graham Hill won only four races that season (eat your heart out, Nigel!), but 42 points was enough to bring the trophy back to Britain for a second time.

Hill recalled that his Dutch GP victory that year was his first World

Last-minute check: Graham Hill in the 1961 BRM

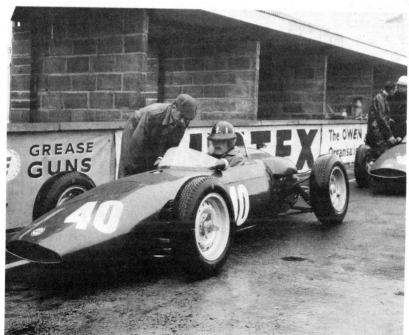

Programmes change as much as faces . . .

Championship win after four years of trying. He went on to win the German and Italian races, and the outcome of the championship was delicately poised. 'As Bette [his wife] had never been to America she came with me to the Grand Prix at Watkins Glen,' he recalled. 'If I won this it meant that I would clinch the World Championship. But Jimmy Clark beat me and that left the title wide open between him and me with everything depending on the final race to be held in South Africa.

'As things turned out I won this last race and emerged as World Champion, and this made me the first British driver ever to win the World Championship in an all-English car – the BRM!'

Graham recalled a less happy occasion in 1962. Despite the fact that the non-championship Easter meeting that year at Goodwood was his first Formula One victory, that particular meeting marked the accident that nearly cost Stirling Moss his life and which *did* cost him his motor-racing career. In his book, *Graham*, he wrote:

'Stirling had made a couple of pit-stops because of problems with his car and lost valuable time. He made a brilliant attempt to get back into the race and broke the course record in doing so. I was leading the race comfortably, with Stirling still two laps behind me – when he flew past on the outside of a bend. Normally Stirling would never have attempted to pass anyone there – and as he overtook me he was already off the track and on the grass and then, for no apparent reason, he just ploughed straight on into the bank.

'The accident was horrific. It took half an hour to cut him out of the wreckage. His face was smashed, his left side paralysed, and he didn't regain consciousness for a month. When he did eventually come round in hospital he couldn't remember a thing – the race or the accident – nor even getting out of bed that morning and going to Goodwood, and it's remained that way ever since.

'Stirling recovered as we all know but the accident ended his racing career as a driver, and that is one of the saddest things that ever happened for the sport. Stirling was one of the greatest drivers the world has ever known.'

Prophetic words indeed because thirteen years later people were saying the same things about Graham himself – killed not on the race-track but in fog approaching Elstree airfield in his plane on a Saturday evening, 29 November 1975. Roger Moody remembers that evening well. He was working at Television Centre on *Match of the Day* when the news was flashed on the teleprinters. 'Were we to give out the news at the end of what was essentially a soccer programme? In the end the production team could not confirm it before the programme came off the air, and Jimmy Hill was spared having to make that awful announcement – but everyone in television sport was shattered. Who could have forgotten those magical moments sparring with Jackie Stewart on *Sports Review of the Year* – let alone the great man's love of driving?' (Incidentally, the final chapter in his book was completed by his widow and the book was published the year after Graham's death. His son Damon is now aiming for the top in the sport his father loved so much, and is currently working his way through the Formula Three scene.)

Graham's great adversary in the sixties was, of course, Jim Clark, and 1963 saw the start of a four-wins-in-a-row sequence of British GPs for Clark. On a blazing summer's day in July he had come to Silverstone with a run of three wins – in Belgium again, Holland and France – behind him. It was his twenty-eighth race, and 1963 was going to be 'his' year and part of a remarkable run of British World Champions – Hill the previous year, Surtees in 1964, Clark again in 1965, and the remarkable Hill taking his second title in 1968 for Lotus after Clark's death.

Clark came to Silverstone, then, in his beloved green Lotus sporting, for the first time, broad yellow speed stripes. You couldn't mistake Colin

Silverstone 1963: the second of Clark's five wins in the British Grand Prix

Chapman's team. But from pole position Clark saw Jack Brabham, Dan Gurney, Bruce McLaren and Graham Hill all blur past him. Not to worry. Clark was third on lap 2, second on lap 3, first on lap 4, and there he stayed for the rest of the seventy-eight laps. Boring? Not a bit of it. This was a demonstration of racing at its highest level, and even with a 35-second lead over Hill with seven laps to go, Clark was having to conserve fuel by cruising round in top gear. The race had been increased to eighty-two laps to ensure that it ran the necessary two hours, but had the Lotus team got its fuel calculations wrong? In the end Clark flashed home but poor Graham Hill, in second place, suddenly found his BRM stuttering at Stowe on the last lap and Surtees scorched past to finish ahead of him. From somewhere a piper had appeared and Silverstone echoed to 'Scotland the Brave' as Clark, Chapman and the Lotus team mechanics took their lap of honour aboard, of all vehicles, a farm trailer.

For the record, Clark in 1963, on his way to the first of his two World Championships, earned seven pole positions out of ten races, six fastest laps and seven wins. He, the rest of the Brits – Surtees, Hill, Peter Arundell, Bob Anderson, Mike Spence, Innes Ireland, Trevor Taylor and

Mike Hailwood – and the country's motor-racing aficionados now looked ahead to 1964 and a new home for the British Grand Prix.

Brands Hatch, sandwiched now by the 'old' A20 trunk road and the 'new' M20 motorway, between Swanley and Wrotham, can claim a racing history as far back as that first Brooklands GP in 1926. But the Kent circuit in those days of the Roaring Twenties started with less of a roar and more of a whisper – cyclists pedalling furiously around the grass bowl provided for their leisure and recreation. In 1928 grass-track motor-cycle racing took over, but not until 1950 and the injection of £17,000 worth of tarmac around a one-mile circuit did car racing come to Brands. A decade later the GP circuit was opened, the track having grown to 2.65 miles, and today that still is just about the length of what many past and present drivers and hundreds of thousands of spectators believe is the most entertaining circuit in the world.

Like Silverstone, Brands Hatch is synonymous with one man. In the Midlands it was the late Jimmy Brown, down south it is John Webb – both keen rivals but both appreciative of the other's success in the tough world of motor-racing.

Brown was around when Silverstone began in 1948 and, until his death in April 1988, was running the business as managing director. Recalling those days forty years ago, Jimmy has been quoted as saying: 'We relied on faith, hope, charity, rope and posts.' How things have changed. In the fifties, motor-racing and Silverstone's sitting tenant, a farmer, endured an uneasy existence alongside each other, with arguments the order of the day. Brown lived through it all: the farmer eventually selling out in 1959; the threat of the siting of London's third airport at Silverstone in the late sixties; the purchase of nearly 400 acres of freehold land from the Ministry of Defence, and a further 240 acres in the seventies, to guarantee the future of the sport. He once even had to deal with a bomb at one of the track's early GPs. It turned out to be a practice dummy, but as one would expect at a military site, live bombs and ammunition had been dumped at what after all was once a bomber airfield.

John Webb, too, has had his trials and tribulations at Brands. At fifty-seven, he has been influential in the commercialisation of British motor-racing for more than twenty years. As he himself says: 'In my early years it fell to me to arrange the sale of Brands Hatch and other circuits to Grovewood Securities, purely to preserve their continuity. It was always my ambition to ensure the circuits [Brands, Oulton and Snetterton] were eventually owned by active motor-racing people, and when during the seventies it was rumoured that a sale was imminent it was actually Angela [Webb's wife and business partner] and myself who were trying to buy them. Twice the money arrangements collapsed at the last moment, and once, when we had the money, it was decided not to sell.'

Ironically a sale eventually went through. Two years ago multi-million-aire computer company boss John Foulston paid £5.25 million for the circuits, with the Webbs' share an agreed twenty per cent (later to rise to thirty per cent) – and operating control.

Perhaps two of John Webb's biggest hurdles to overcome were the deal that gave the British GP to Silverstone for five years up to and including 1991, and the death of Foulston in September 1987 while testing one of his beloved racing cars at, ironically, Silverstone. Today Webb is Chairman of Brands Hatch Circuits Ltd and a man with a mission to succeed as much in the future as he has in the past – a past that goes back to that first Brands Hatch British GP in 1964.

Unlike Silverstone's entry onto the World Championship stage fourteen years before, Brands saw race day break damp and overcast, and the anticipated 130,000-strong crowd did not materialise. What *did* materialise was a Clark/Hill/Surtees 1–2–3 for Lotus/BRM/Ferrari. By the end of the year there was a role reversal with Surtees leading Hill and Clark home in the drivers' championship and Ferrari leading BRM and Lotus in the constructors' championship. But Brands was born and on its way and if Hill had little chance of catching Clark up front for the entire distance the Kent circuit was now on the map.

From then until 1987 Brands and Silverstone alternated as the venue for the British GP. In those years the Kent circuit has seen only two British winners (Clark in 1964 and Mansell in 1986) to Silverstone's seven (Clark in 1965 and 1967, Stewart in 1969 and 1971, Hunt in 1977, Watson in 1981 and Mansell in 1987).

Back at Silverstone for the 1965 GP the old firm of Clark and Hill were repeating their usual one-two scenario and, if the Flying Scotsman was on the way to his second World Championship title, a new, young pretender from north of the border was already beginning to make his presence felt.

John Young Stewart made his British GP debut at Silverstone that year, and just to point the way to the future squeezed himself onto the front row of the four-car grid and a fifth-place finish (to add to his first-ever Formula One win at the same track in the International Trophy race earlier that same year). The son of a garage owner, Jackie Stewart first found fame as a marksman and nearly made the Olympics, but preferred four wheels to a gun barrel (although he's made up for it since with his clay-pigeon shoot at Gleneagles). The choice proved correct. Stewart's then record twenty-seven wins came from only ninety-nine races. His

Opposite *The young pretender: John Young Stewart, 1965*

three World Championship victories in 1969, 1971 and 1973 and his astute commercial sense have brought the Dumbarton boy fame and wealth – and friends from racing mechanics to royalty.

The return to Brands Hatch in 1966 was also publicised as 'the Return of Power'. The 16 July race was the first British GP to be run under the new 3-litre Formula. The event lived up to tradition – dull, overcast, and a shower just before the flag which meant even more fun for the teams already waging a tyre war involving Goodyear, Dunlop and Firestone. And if that wasn't enough, practice wasn't made perfect by the presence of Hollywood director John Frankenheimer, star James Garner and an entire film crew shooting scenes for the movie *Grand Prix*. Whilst Jack Brabham and Denny Hulme dominated qualifying, more than a little additional interest was provided by Sweden's Joakim Bonnier running his Brabham and Mike Spence his Lotus dressed up and painted red to look like Ferraris!

The hero of the 1966 race – and the year – was Jack Brabham. Already twice World Champion, in 1959 and 1960 in a Cooper Climax, Jack was on the way to a hat-trick of titles but this time in his own car. When he won the preceding French GP at Rheims it was the first-ever victory by a driver in a car bearing his own name.

The last three British GPs of the sixties are notable for some good and some not-so-good memories. In 1967 Clark added his fifth, and what was to be his final, British victory to his ultimate tally of twenty-five wins. Nobody that overcast July day at Silverstone realised that it was to be the last time the Scot would be seen racing on British shores. The following year – and Brands – saw the face of traditional motor-racing disappear for ever. Graham Hill, by now with Lotus, was leading the Norwich team following the desperate Formula Two accident at Hockenheim in April which cost Jim Clark his life. Hill and team-mate Jackie Oliver swept into view not in British Racing Green but in the red, white and gold colours of their financial backer. Gold Leaf Team Lotus was born and big sponsorship, now twenty years old in motor-racing, had arrived. But the race was won by Jo Siffert in another Lotus.

The decade ended where it began, at Silverstone, with Stewart winning his first British GP (despite a heavy crash in practice), on the way to his first world title later that year. Incidentally it was also the year that nearly saw Graham Hill forced out of motor-racing. The collapse of a rear tyre at Watkins Glen in the penultimate race of the season saw his Lotus crash, leaving him with a broken right knee and a dislocated left. Despite warnings that he might never walk properly again, let alone drive, he was back behind the wheel for the first GP of the 1970 season, at Kyalami, almost five months to the day after his American 'incident'. Apparently

James Garner (second from left) *during filming of John Frankenheimer's* Grand Prix *at Brands Hatch in 1966*

heroin proved more beneficial than normal pain-killers during his hospitalisation – as did champagne and pheasant sent by friends and fans!

Hill was also the highest-placed home-grown driver at Brands in July in sixth place. The race was won by Austrian Jochen Rindt, who became the first posthumous World Champion when he was tragically killed in practice at Monza for the Italian GP.

If the sixties belonged to Clark, the seventies – or at least 1971–3 – belonged to Stewart. As reigning champion he had ended 1970 in, for him, a lowly fifth place, although he was still the highest-placed British driver that year. But in 1971 he was about to bounce back and claim his title. Silverstone that year is remembered for little but the beginning and end of the event. The race starter began to drop his flag, spotted some of the cars edging forward, and hesitated with the Union Jack. By then some of the drivers had started, some had actually stopped. By the time the flag *was* dropped, cars were smashing into each other at the back – but up front the grid got away, with Stewart in third place. By lap 4, out of sixty-eight, he was away in front. It was his second British GP victory.

If the sponsorship of the race at Silverstone in 1971 by the International Wool Secretariat infuriated the purists, the 1972 takeover by tobacco upset even more people. The race was to be known as the John Player Grand Prix, the cigarette manufacturers having decided to extend their support of Lotus, under the Gold Leaf banner, to take in the country's top motor race. In the event at least the sponsors were happy, for the Brands Hatch GP was won by Emerson Fittipaldi in his John Player Special, which of course the year before had been a Lotus – and still was!

If the records show that Jackie only managed second place in the title chase in 1972 (to Fittipaldi), but recaptured his crown before his eventual retirement in 1973, the statistics also point out the beginning of a series of British Grand Prix mishaps, which started in that Silverstone race of 1973. Throughout the fifties and the sixties there had, tragically, been races with fatalities, races stopped or interrupted before the normal finish, and races with major pile-ups. But not at the British Grand Prix. Not until now.

In 1973 nine out of the twenty-eight cars starting the Silverstone race were involved in the biggest accident ever seen at a British GP. On lap 2 fourth-placed Jody Scheckter unwittingly began the mayhem by trying to overtake, spinning into the pit wall and bouncing back into the oncoming traffic – including the cars of British drivers Roger Williamson and Mike Hailwood. Fortunately the most severe injury was a broken ankle suffered by Andrea de Adamich in his Brabham, but it spelt the end of the Italian's Grand Prix career. Peter Revson won the restarted race – and his first GP victory, thus achieving a ten-year-old ambition – with an emerging youngster, James Hunt, taking fourth place in only his third GP. Watch this space.

If 1973 had seen possible driver error, it was nothing to compare with the organisational bunglings at Brands in 1974. Another emerging white hope – or rather *red* hope in the form of Ferrari's Niki Lauda – had taken pole and had led for most of the seventy-five laps. But a tyre blow-out eventually forced him into the pits on the penultimate lap. When he tried to exit the pit-lane stewards, hangers-on and even a course car blocked his way, as officials waited to flag home Jody Scheckter in first place regardless of the possible re-entry into the race of other competitors. A Ferrari appeal eventually gained Lauda fifth place instead of his original ninth, and red faces all round for the British organisers.

Interest in the 1975 race had already started earlier in the year with Silverstone introducing a chicane at Woodcote, Graham Hill announcing his retirement shortly before the meeting, and Master James now in the

Opposite Jim Clark at Silverstone for his last GP win in Britain, 1967, with (top) *Colin Chapman in the foreground*

first full year of a brand-new car – the Hesketh. Surely 1975 was going to be a clean race. But this was Britain and this was summer. Practice had offered a warning to those prepared to listen: Thursday's thunderstorms had caused power cuts; Saturday's race was not going to escape. By two-thirds' distance the heavens had opened, the circuit was flooding, and the best drivers in the world suddenly found themselves unable to control their dry-tyred cars. Into the barriers and each other careered car after car. Out came a red flag at Woodcote as twelve cars discovered wings of a water variety would have been more in order as their race came to an end. Race leader Fittipaldi, who seconds before had popped into the pits, now exited with wet-weather tyres to find the race stopped and himself the surprised winner, with only fifty-six out of the scheduled sixty-seven laps completed. It had to get better, surely?

James Hunt had made his fond farewells to Lord Hesketh at the end of the year and now, in 1976, was driving a McLaren. With four pole positions and two wins, in Spain and France, already behind him, he and everyone else had high hopes of an Englishman (as opposed to a Scotsman) winning the British GP for the first time since Peter Collins eighteen years before. Television pictures and still photographs have captured for ever that first-bend incident which involved four cars – including Hunt's. Who was to blame paled into insignificance as it was announced that the restarted race would not include James, who was said to have infringed the rules. The baying of the British crowd convinced the officials that they were wrong and he was allowed to restart the race – which he went on to win. But the old enemy was not to be outdone. Ferrari inevitably appealed, and two months later Hunt was disqualified and Lauda promoted from second to first place. Justice, however, was seen to be done when, in that rain-soaked end-of-season race at Mount Fuji in Japan, James clinched the title by one point from Niki.

If the British GP four-year run of bad luck changed in 1977, so did it for the reigning World Champion. Hunt clinched victory at Silverstone to become only the second British driver, after Jackie Stewart in 1971, to win his home race in the seventies. He also took pole and fastest lap, but at the season's end could not stave off Lauda from regaining the crown he held in 1975 and had so reluctantly relinquished in 1976.

As the decade drew towards a close British television at last came to terms with the unrelenting march of the sponsors and re-entered the high-speed world of Formula One in 1978. Too late, though, to see a British winner, only the popular Ulsterman John Watson managing third at Brands in 1978 behind Argentinian Carlos Reutemann, and fourth at Silverstone the next year behind Switzerland's Clay Regazzoni. The world titles were taken by American Mario Andretti and South African

Above *Silverstone 1975: James Hunt leads Emerson Fittipaldi*

Below *Brands Hatch a year later: Hunt (foreground)* and the notorious shunt

Jody Scheckter respectively, the latter the last World Champion to drive for Ferrari.

In 1980 the immensely likeable Alan Jones took the title back to Australia for the first time since Jack Brabham fourteen years before. He also won the British GP at Brands, driving for Williams who took the constructors' title for the first time. They retained it in 1981 (and took it again in 1986 and 1987), but 1981 was Watty's year. John Watson's Silverstone win was even more popular than it would normally have been, since he was the only driver flying the home flag, Brian Henton and Derek Warwick in their Tolemans and Nigel Mansell in the Lotus having failed to qualify. He responded in just 1 hour 27 minutes, pushing Reutemann into second place. Nelson Piquet was out of the points but took the first of his three world titles that year.

For Watson the next season was the most frustrating of his career. Although the great years of British GP wins for Lauda and Prost were upon us, John was poised at season's end in Las Vegas to take the world crown, *provided* the points distribution favoured him and not his closest rivals. At the end he could only manage to finish second and the title went to fifth-placed Finn, Keke Rosberg, who won only one GP in his title year – and only five throughout his career. Perhaps he, along with Prost and Piquet in 1986 and 1987, were all blessed with the good luck that must go with the consistency of a World Champion's year.

Brands Hatch 1983: Niki Lauda takes the spoils

Niki Lauda, so long a favourite with the appreciative UK fans, had surprisingly come good in 1982 to win only his second British GP. As before he took the Brands Hatch chequered flag – although this time in a McLaren and not a Ferrari. He and arch-rival but great friend Alain Prost – the Professor – were to alternate the winning of the British race from 1982 to 1985.

Silverstone in 1983 passed off quietly enough (with Prost winning from Piquet), but in 1984 the jinx returned and another three-in-a-row British GPs were to be marred by controversy. Reigning World Champion Nelson Piquet and the Professor lined up on the front row of the 1983 Brands grid, and the enthusiastic crowd craned forward as the red light sparkled to green to start the seventy-one lap race. Not one lap had been completed before Italian veteran Riccardo Patrese in his Alfa caused team-mate Eddie Cheever, Philippe Alliot in the Ram, Stefan Johansson in the Tyrrell and Jo Gartner in the Osella to have, in the quaint words of the Formula One world, 'a coming-together'. A five-nation, four-car débâcle (Patrese escaped the mayhem). Not to be outdone, on lap 10 Britain's Dr Jonathan Palmer decided to join the United Nations, and his Ram team-mate, at the same spot. Enough was enough and the red flag was out on the next lap.

Once the wreckage had been cleared Niki Lauda and McLaren polished off the restarted race – minus four of the original laps – beating off

Brands again, 1984: first-lap frolics

the challenge of Britain's Derek Warwick in a Renault, and going on to take his third and McLaren's second world titles.

Silverstone notched up a not-so-notable first the following year when, with Prost exiting from Woodcote for the last but one time, an over-enthusiastic and still undisclosed official brought the chequered flag down. Only sixty-five laps of a sixty-six-lap race had been completed. Fortunately for Alain he led by over a lap at the time and no one protested. The hapless start-line clerk is the only man in the history of the World Championship to end a race in that manner. No wonder he has gone to ground. Meanwhile the Professor went on to take the first of his two back-to-back world titles.

Then 1986, and back to Brands and mayhem. The no-love-lost partnership of Piquet and Mansell were alongside each other on the grid, while Frenchman Jacques Laffite was equalling Graham Hill's all-time record of 176 GP starts. The race lasted as far as the first corner. A massive pile-up saw the unfortunate Laffite out of the race, together with Christian Danner, Piercarlo Ghinzani and Allen Berg. Laffite has still to return to his Formula One seat. For Mansell, whose drive-shaft coupling exploded on the grid, the restarted race was a blessing in disguise. The Isle of Man driver leapt into Piquet's spare car, and to add insult to injury pipped his favourite Brazilian into second place by just 5.574 seconds.

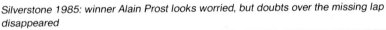

Silverstone 1985: winner Alain Prost looks worried, but doubts over the missing lap disappeared

BRANDS HATCH

DRUIDS

PADDOCK

SILVERSTONE

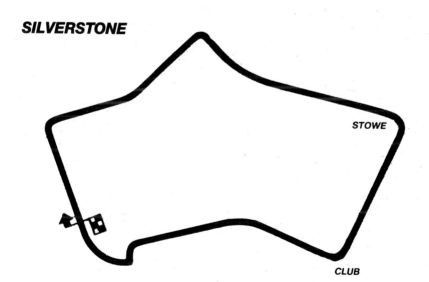

STOWE

CLUB

No victory was sweeter, for this was Nigel's first British GP win, although he had won at the same track the previous October when a splendidly organised last-minute Grand Prix of Europe was awarded to the Kent track. How Nigel's year and his World Championship title hopes ended in Australia is now just another statistic, even if his exploding Goodyear tyre provided one of the sporting pictures of the year. That's motor-racing.

So to Silverstone for 1987 when the Northamptonshire circuit came of age. How come? The 1987 British GP was the twenty-first World Championship race to be held at the track since that May day in 1950.

And what a way to celebrate. The old Williams firm were up front again, and apart from a cheeky if short-lived intrusion from the Professor, that's the way it stayed until Nigel took the flag again from Nelson. But what drama lay behind that victory – and for Mansell it was a drama of tyres once again. With thirty-five laps gone and with Piquet able to draw away from him, Mansell gambled on new rubber. Piquet elected to stay as he was. Thirty laps lay ahead and nearly half a minute separated the two rivals. Could Nigel catch Nelson? And if he could, could he get past in time?

Catch he did. 'I drove the last twenty laps at ten tenths, right on the limit. I don't really like to do that on such a quick circuit but I knew that was what it was going to take to beat Nelson,' said Nigel later. With the crowd willing him on he dummied and then swept past the Brazilian with just two laps to go. Just under six miles of a 193-mile race left. The scenes after Mansell took that chequered flag were reminiscent of that first non-championship Grand Prix back in 1948 when the spectators crowded on to the circuit. Nigel ran out of fuel on the wind-down lap, and couldn't resist stopping his lift for a quick kiss of the ground where he had passed Piquet. A fitting end to a sensational Silverstone celebration.

Even as the British basked in Nigel's glory, once again his cruel luck was to turn against him. Engine and mechanical problems in the second half of the season placed him in a position where he had to win the last two races to clinch the championship. Perhaps trying just too hard in practice in Japan, he crashed and was ruled out for the remainder of the season. And if that was not enough, Nelson clinched the title with a season's performance that one can only generously describe, in comparison with his team-mate's, as adequate.

But if there was only one highlight of 1987 it had to be Silverstone – and the Shell Oils British Grand Prix – where the whole story began when the first chapter of the Formula One World Championship was written thirty-seven years before.

Complete results of the British GPs can be found on pages 168–71.

It's all in the hands: Eddie Cheever (top) and Stefano Modena

Drivers are as declared at the beginning of the 1988 season. Statistics are correct to the end of 1987. Abbreviations are listed on p. 167.

NELSON PIQUET   No. 1

Lotus-Honda
Born   17.8.52   Brazilian
GPs contested   141
Best results
  Wins   20
  1980 USAW, HOL, ITA; 1981 ARG, RMS, GER; 1982 CAN; 1983 BRE, ITA, EUR; 1984 CAN, USAE; 1985 FRA; 1986 BRE, GER, HON, ITA; 1987 GER, HON, ITA.
  2nd 19; *3rd* 11; *4th* 10; *5th* 5; *6th* 3
WC placings
  1979 15th (3 points); 1980 2nd (54); 1981 1st (50); 1982 11th (20); 1983 1st (59); 1984 5th (29); 1985 8th (21); 1986 3rd (69); 1987 1st (73 [76])

Three times World Champion, Nelson Piquet joins that élite group of Brabham, Stewart and Lauda who have scored a hat-trick of titles, but says, at 35, that he cannot better the all-time record of five titles set by Fangio in the 1950s.

Divorced, with one child, Piquet lives in Monaco. He was the Brazilian Formula Super Vee champion in 1976 and made his F1 debut in 1978 in an Ensign. He has also driven for McLaren, Brabham (his first two titles), and of course Williams (his last title), before somewhat controversially joining Lotus from 1988 onwards.

James Hunt's verdict: Piquet won his third World Championship after a not very good driving season. It doesn't often happen like that. He was certainly lucky. There were really only the two Williams drivers in the race in 1987. Piquet made an awful lot of elementary mistakes as well as being noticeably slower than Mansell all season. In defence of his slowness, he kept saying all along that he was being more consistent but he was mighty lucky. He made mistakes in the French GP, was off the road in the Spanish race, delayed himself in pit stops and one way or another drove like a beginner – and still emerged as champion. He had to be lucky, and Nigel deserved the title more than Nelson.

SATORU NAKAJIMA   No. 2

Lotus–Honda
Born   23.2.53   Japanese
GPs contested   16
Best results
   4th 1; *5th* 1; *6th* 2
WC placings
   1987 11th (7 points)

Nakajima lives in Walton-on-Thames, but his origins are in Japan. Aged 35, he began racing in karts, progressing through saloon cars, F2, F3, F3000 and Le Mans. He owes his chance in GP racing to Honda, who stipulated for 1987 that Lotus must give him a drive if the English team wanted the Japanese engine. Satoru, who tested the Williams Honda extensively some years back, managed to finish 11th in 1987 mainly due to the chassis he sat in and the engine that propelled him.

James Hunt's verdict: He's out of his depth in F1 cars. He's not competent and it's unfair of Honda to have put him in that position. The kindest thing they could do would be to park him quietly in a siding or send him back to Japan and let him do domestic racing.

JONATHAN PALMER   No. 3

Tyrrell–Cosworth
Born   7.11.56   British
GPs contested   55
Best results
   4th 1; *5th* 2
WC placings
   1987 11th (7 points)

Born in London, and married in 1987, 31-year-old Palmer was British F3 champion in 1981 and European F2 champion in 1983 – the year he made his F1 debut with a one-off drive for Williams at the Brands Hatch GP of Europe. There followed three unproductive years, at RAM in 1984 and Zakspeed in 1985–6, before he swapped seats with Martin Brundle and joined Tyrrell.
   The Reading-based driver immediately found success with Tyrrell, winning his first F1 World

Championship – the Jim Clark Cup for drivers of normally-aspirated cars – while clinching, with team-mate Philippe Streiff, the Colin Chapman Cup for the top constructor of non-turbo cars for Tyrrell. He hates wasting time: together with motor-racing and his wife, jetting around in helicopters is another love of his life.

James Hunt's verdict: He did a very good job in 1987, very steady. He got the Tyrrell round to the finish and deservedly won his class. How good he will be at the top level again when everybody is normally aspirated is very much an open question – assuming, of course, that Ken Tyrrell can produce a competitive car. Palmer is tough, strong and determined, so let's hope he can deliver the goods in a motor to rival the best.

at Brands Hatch – under the eagle eye of Ken Tyrrell himself. This seat alongside the normally-aspirated World Champion is a huge opportunity for the popular 'Julio'.

James Hunt's verdict: He obviously has ability. He showed good form towards the end of the 1987 season in F3000. His Brands Hatch win, though, is hardly a pointer to the future. A win on the continent would have been a better guide to form.

JULIAN BAILEY   No. 4

Tyrell–Cosworth
Born   9.10.61   British
GPs contested   0

Started in Formula Ford at the tender age of 17 but had to wait until 1982 to make his mark with a national championship in FF1600 and victory in the prestigious Formula Ford Festival. Julian next spent a few fairly barren years in FF2000 and F3, but worked hard to get into F3000 in 1987 and was rewarded with a stunning victory

NIGEL MANSELL   No. 5

Williams–Judd
Born   8.8.54   British
GPs contested   104
Best results
   Wins   13
   1985 EUR, SA; 1986 BEL, CAN, FRA, GB, POR; 1987 RSM, FRA, GB, AUT, ESP, MEX
   2nd 3; *3rd* 8; *4th* 5; *5th* 6; *6th* 8
WC placings
   1981 14th (8 points); 1982 14th (7); 1983 12th (10); 1984 9th (13); 1985 6th (31); 1986 2nd (70 [72]); 1987 2nd (61)

Perhaps the unluckiest driver in 1986/87: the World Championship was his but for a blow-out in Australia one year and a crash in practice in Japan the next.

Mansell confounds his critics with unpredictable behaviour off the track from time to time, and superb skills and determination on it. He started his motor-racing career in Formula Ford, followed with not much more success in F3 and F2, but got his big chance when Colin Chapman took a gamble and gave him a F1 seat in 1980, his first race being the Austrian GP. Now in his ninth season, Nigel has remained loyal to only two teams – Lotus (1980–4) and Williams (1985–   ).

James Hunt's verdict: There's no doubt that he is very fast, very tough and very determined. He put it over Piquet all the time in 1987, but it seems to have taken its toll on him, both physically and mentally. He's had and blown two chances and you don't often get more than that in this life. But for 1988 the pressure on him will be considerably eased. Last year he had physical problems coping with the turbocharged car, but the atmosphere car should be a lot easier. Also, expectations of his chances are not so high which should ease the mental strain. But, contrary to popular belief, I think the atmosphere cars will be competitive over the course of the season and no doubt Mansell will be the top atmosphere driver and could well win the Championship.

RICCARDO PATRESE   *No. 6*

Williams–Judd
Born   17.4.54   Italian
GPs contested   160
Best results
  Wins   2
  1982 MON; 1983 SA
  2nd 4; *3rd* 5; *4th* 2; *5th* 3; *6th* 7
WC placings
  1977 19th (1 point); 1978 11th
  (11); 1979 19th (2); 1980 9th
  (/); 1981 11th (10); 1982 10th
  (21); 1983 9th (13); 1984 13th
  (8); 1986 15th (2); 1987 13th
  (6)

If there is one title that 34-year-old Padova-born Patrese can claim, it is that he is the most experienced GP driver currently doing the rounds. He has 160 races behind him since his debut at Monaco in 1977 – only Graham Hill and Jacques Laffite (176) and Niki Lauda (171) have more.

Happily married to Suzy, with three children, Riccardo commutes between his two homes, in Padova and Monaco, between racing. He won the karting world championship in 1975 and the European F3 championship the next year. His 1977 F1 debut was with Shadow, followed by four years at Arrows (1978–81), two years at Brabham (1982–3), two years at Alfa-Romeo (1984–5) and two more years at Brabham (1986–7). He should prove more of a stable companion for Mansell at Williams than Piquet was, and possibly less of a rival on and off the track. He lists model trains amongst his hobbies – and says he dislikes liars!

James Hunt's verdict: He's been around a long time now – probably too long! He's pretty quick and was pretty competitive when he and Piquet were at Brabham together. Riccardo is a bit unpredictable, though, in overtaking and things like that – he always has been – but he's better now than he used to be. His big chance comes in 1988 being lined up alongside Mansell in the Williams team.

PIERCARLO GHINZANI   No. 9

Zakspeed
Born   16.1.52   Italian
GPs contested   65
Best results
   5th 1
WC placings
   1984 19th (2 points)

Not one of the younger drivers on the GP scene, but one of the least successful. Now 36, he lives in Bergamo and Monte Carlo; he likes bodybuilding and hates rugby and American football. After winning the Italian F2 championship in 1979, he

debuted in F1 with Osella in the Belgian GP in 1981 and, apart from seven races with Toleman in 1985, stayed at the Torino-based team until 1987 when he joined Ligier.

James Hunt's verdict: He never seems to have had the machinery for one to be able to make a fair judgement of his ability.

BERND SCHNEIDER   No. 10

Zakspeed
Born   20.7.65   German
GPs contested   0

German F3 champion in 1987, he is seen as the man most likely to erase the unhappy memory of the deaths of fellow-countrymen Stefan Bellof and Manfred Winkelhock in 1985. He started racing karts in 1976, winning the world junior title in 1980, and graduated to single-seater racing in 1984. Success in all categories would have led logically to F3000, but along came Zakspeed for 1988. Bernd's idol was the late Ronnie Peterson.

James Hunt's verdict: He would appear to have the ability and makings of a GP driver but has taken a huge step back in his career by driving for Zakspeed when he could have perfected his craft first by taking up the offer of a F3000 drive for 1988. He will have a lot of work to undo the situation he now finds himself in.

ALAIN PROST   No. 11

McLaren–Honda
Born   24.2.55   French
GPs contested   121
Best results
   Wins   28
   1981 FRA, HOL, ITA; 1982 SA, BRE; 1983 FRA, BEL, GB, AUT; 1984 BRE, RSM, MON, GER, HOL, EUR, POR; 1985 BRE, MON, GB, AUT, ITA; 1986 RSM, MON, AUT, AUS; 1987 BRE, BEL, POR
   2nd 14; *3rd* 13; *4th* 4; *5th* 2; *6th* 7
WC placings
   1980 15th (5 points); 1981 5th (43); 1982 4th (34); 1983 2nd

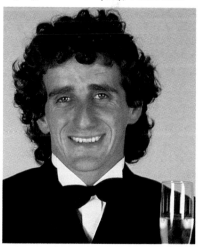

(57); 1984 2nd (71.5); 1985 1st (73 [76]); 1986 1st (72 [[74]); 1987 4th (46)

The Professor is one of the nicest men ever to wear racing overalls. He is also one of the greatest drivers. France's first-ever World Champion also goes into the record books as the holder of the highest number of GP wins – 28 by the end of 1987. The diminutive 33-year-old has won the championship twice since making his F1 debut with McLaren in the 1980 Argentine GP. Before that he was European F3 champion. He drove for Renault 1981–3, but otherwise has always been with McLaren. He lives near Lausanne, likes golf, and says his favourite drivers are Jackie Stewart, whose record number of wins he passed in 1987, and Niki Lauda, his old McLaren team-mate who beat him to the title by just half a point in 1984.

James Hunt's verdict: I think he's the best in the business at the moment. It'll be very interesting to see how he and Ayrton Senna shape up in comparison to each other in the McLaren team. It will be an exciting challenge for Prost to have someone as good as Senna lined up with him. Prost is the ultimate craftsman, he gets the job done. He's very quick, very consistent. His race craft and tactics are pretty much unreachable. He is the top man.

AYRTON SENNA   *No. 12*

McLaren–Honda
Born   21.3.60   Brazilian
GPs contested   62
Best results
  Wins   6
  1985 POR, BEL; 1986 ESP, USAE; 1987 MON, USAE
  2nd 11; *3rd* 8; *4th* 2; *5th* 3; *6th* 2
WC placings
  1984 9th (13 points); 1985 4th (38); 1986 4th (55); 1987 3rd (57)

Ayrton Senna Da Silva probably has his best chance of success in the McLaren team from 1988. Born in São Paulo, the 28-year-old Brazilian lives there – and in Esher, South London. Runner-up in the karting world champion-ships in 1979 and 1980, he was British Formula Ford champion in 1981, British and European champion in 1982, and British F3 champion in 1983. He made his

entry into F1 in the 1984 Brazilian GP with Toleman, then spent three years with Lotus before switching to McLaren. In only sixty-two races he has had sixteen pole positions (the same as Prost) and six wins. *The* man to watch.

James Hunt's verdict: In 1986 Senna really threw a lot of chances away, and made a lot of mistakes by working on the basis that you drive flat out at all times. However, in 1987 he worked out that that wasn't the way to do things and was a very different animal. In the two races that he won in 1987 – two street races – he really used his head very well and basically outfumbled everybody.

PHILIPPE STREIFF No. 14

AGS–Cosworth
Born 26.6.55 French
GPs contested 38
Best results
 3rd 1; 4th 1; 5th 1; 6th 2
WC placings
 1985 15th (4 points); 1986 13th (3); 1987 14th (4)

You cannot take it seriously when Philippe Streiff says he doèsn't like getting up early in the morning to go motor-racing – he's been doing that for 11 years, the last five in F1. Born in Grenoble, the likeable 32-year-old lives in Switzerland with his wife Renée and their two children and enjoys skiing and water-skiing. French F3 champion in 1981, after one F1 race for Renault in 1984 (Portugal) and four for Ligier in 1985 he joined Tyrrell before moving to the French AGS team he first drove for in F2.

James Hunt's verdict: Streiff and Jonathan Palmer were very evenly matched for speed in 1987 in the Tyrrell team. The same really applies to Streiff as it does to Palmer – I put them very much in the same bracket. It remains to be seen how good they will be when the sport is more competitive with all the motors normally aspirated.

MAURICIO GUGELMIN No. 15

March–Judd
Born 20.4.63 Brazilian
GPs contested 0

Came to Britain in 1982, joining
the works Van Diemen team in
FF1600 and promptly becoming
British Champion. Two seasons
in FF2000 followed, and Mauricio
took the European title in 1984.
Graduating to F3 with West
Surrey Racing in 1985, he
clinched the British Championship in the final round. Has spent
two seasons in F3000, finishing
12th and 4th overall and winning
the 1987 series opener at
Silverstone. He and his wife Stella
live in Esher.

James Hunt's verdict: A terribly
charming guy – both on and off
the track. The trouble is he lets
drivers pass him, charmingly, on
the circuits!

IVAN CAPELLI No. 16

March–Judd
Born 24.5.63 Italian
GPs contested 19
Best results
  4th 1; 6th 1
WC placings
  1985 17th (3 points); 1987
19th (1)

The 24-year-old Italian made his
big break into F1 when a Tyrrell
seat became available in the
1985 GP of Europe at Brands
Hatch after the death of Stefan
Bellof. His only other drive for
Tyrrell that year was in Australia
when he finished 4th. He drove
twice for AGS in 1986, but

consolidated his F1 role in 1987
with March, who were returning
after a long absence. He had

previously been Italian F3 champion in 1983, European F3 champion in 1984, and Intercontinental F3000 champion in 1986. He lives in Milan.

James Hunt's verdict: He's pretty good and pretty talented. The 1988 season will be an important year for him when there are more normally-aspirated cars and they will be in a more competitive class.

DEREK WARWICK   *No. 17*

Arrows–Megatron
Born   27.8.54   British
GPs contested   84
Best results
   2nd 2; *3rd* 2; *4th* 3; *5th* 4; *6th* 3
WC placings
   1983 14th (9 points); 1984 7th (23); 1985 13th (5); 1987 16th (3)

Probably Britain's 'forgotten' racing driver, Warwick, at 33, has never really achieved what he thought he might. After struggling with Toleman from 1981–3, the big break came – or so everyone thought – when he joined Renault in 1984. But his two seasons there ended with the demise of the marque, no points for Warwick and no drive for 1986. However, when the popular Elio De Angelis died after an accident while testing in May 1986, Warwick was snapped up for the vacant Brabham seat, but still fared no better. In 1987 he joined

another 'old hand', Eddie Cheever, in the Arrows team and his luck changed – a little.

A native of Alresford near Colchester, Derek lives with his wife Rhonda and their two children in Jersey. He was 1972 world stock-car champion, 1976 European Formula Ford champion, 1978 Vanderwall F3 champion, and runner-up in the European F2 championship in 1980, before breaking into F1 at Las Vegas in 1981. He likes pleasant company, but not some of the people 'he has to suffer in the GP world'.

James Hunt's verdict: He had a pretty much up-and-down season in 1987. A lot of mechanical trouble with the car. He certainly underlined the fact that he's a very competent No. 2 driver. He hasn't really had the opportunity to prove in a competitive car whether he's a number one driver and a potential champion. Time is beginning to run short for him – he's been around a long time. He needs a good season with good results pretty soon if he is going to get a decent career out of F1.

EDDIE CHEEVER   No. 18

Arrows–Megatron
Born   10.1.58   American
GPs contested   102
Best results
   2nd 2; *3rd* 5; *4th* 5; *5th* 3; *6th* 5
WC placings
   1981 11th (10 points); 1982 12th (15); 1983 6th (22); 1984 16th (3); 1987 10th (8)

The only Yank in the pack and a driver who shares with James Hunt the distinction of having driven a Hesketh – back in 1978. The 30-year-old lives in Rome and, inevitably, Monte Carlo. Having won the European and Italian karting titles, he drove in Formula Ford and F3 in 1975, F2 in 1977 when he was European runner-up, and eventually secured a more-or-less permanent F1 drive in 1980 with Osella. Seasons followed with

Tyrrell (1981), Ligier (1982), Renault (1983), Alfa-Romeo (1984–5), one race for Lola (1986), and Arrows (1987). At the same time he shared with Derek Warwick in Jaguar's attempt at the world sports car title in 1986, and doubled up in that Formula with his GP racing in 1987.

James Hunt's verdict: He's been around an awfully long time to have done nothing in F1. He's pretty quick and drives hard, but I don't think he's ever going to make it to the very top.

ALESSANDRO NANNINI
No. 19

Benetton–Ford
Born   7.7.59   Italian
GPs contested   31

The 28-year-old Italian lives in Siena and not unnaturally declares that Monza and Imola are his favourite tracks. He also lists sun, sleeping and swimming among his likes – and work as something he hates! That could explain why, since his debut in

1986, he has yet to get in the points, although to be fair his car, the Minardi, was not one you would expect to find near the front. He began in motocross, before going rallying, Formula Abarth, F2 and sports car racing.

James Hunt's verdict: He showed really very good form in a not very good car. Of course, you can't really make an accurate assessment of someone until they are in a really competitive car alongside another competitive driver. I would expect Nannini to go pretty well in the future. He's got plenty of experience and driving for Benetton is his big chance.

THIERRY BOUTSEN *No. 20*

Benetton–Ford
Born 13.7.57 Belgian
GPs contested 73
Best results
   2nd 1; *3rd* 1; *4th* 3; *5th* 5; *6th* 3
WC placings
   1984 14th (5 points); 1985 11th (11); 1987 8th (16)

Another driver who prefers to keep his money in Monaco, the 30-year-old Belgian has improved steadily since he stepped into an Arrows car at his home GP in 1983. Before that he had performed well in F2. In 1987 he joined Benetton, finishing in the points six times.

James Hunt's verdict: Boutsen I find a little enigmatic. He's certainly a very competent GP

driver. Whether or not he's a top-class No. 1 I can't tell as he was with Teo Fabi at Benetton who wasn't a top driver. It will be interesting to compare him with his new team-mate, Alessandro Nannini.

NICOLA LARINI *No. 21*

Osella–Alfa-Romeo
Born 19.5.64 Italian
GPs contested 1

The 24-year-old, one of twelve Italians to take part in F1 in 1987, was the youngest driver on the GP circuit. He failed to qualify his Coloni at Monza and retired on

lap 9 in Spain. He was Italian F3 champion in 1986.

James Hunt's verdict: I know nothing about him.

ANDREA DE CESARIS   *No. 22*

Rial–Cosworth
Born   31.5.59   Italian
GPs contested   104
Best results
   2nd 2; 3rd 2; 4th 2; 5th 1; 6th 3
WC placings
   1981 18th (1 point); 1982 17th (5); 1983 8th (15); 1984 16th (3); 1985 17th (3); 1987 14th (4)

Now 28, Andrea was even known as de Crasharis at one time because of his continued efforts to wrap his car around the nearest armco! After making his F1 debut for Alfa-Romeo in Canada in 1980, he spent a year with McLaren before returning to Alfa until 1983. Two years at Ligier followed, with 1986 spent with Minardi and 1987 with Brabham. Andrea doesn't like being away from his home in Rome for too long.

James Hunt's verdict: Like Philippe Alliot, de Cesaris has difficulty in keeping the car on the road. He's quick whilst he's on the track, but he's not someone the teams queue up to sign. I don't think he's got a big future at all.

ADRIAN CAMPOS   *No. 23*

Minardi–Cosworth
Born   17.6.60   Spanish
GPs contested   15

Another driver said to have clinched his place in F1 by bringing vast sponsorship with him, the 27-year-old Spaniard from Valencia does not have a brilliant pre-GP career behind him. He drove in the European F3 championship in 1984, the German F3 series in 1985, and dipped his foot in F3000 in 1986.

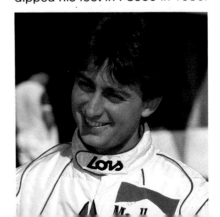

$1 million is said to have clinched his place in the Minardi team in 1987, but he achieved nothing, finishing only once (last in Spain) and being disqualified in Brazil for not observing start procedure.

James Hunt's verdict: Out of his depth in an F1 car and shouldn't be in one.

LUIS PEREZ SALA *No. 24*

Minardi–Cosworth
Born 15.5.59 Spanish
GPs contested 0

European Alfa Sprint champion in 1983, the Barcelona driver moved into F3 for 1984–5, scoring a win at Varano, then stepped up to F3000 in 1986. He won at Enna and in the inaugural

Birmingham Superprix on the way to 4th place overall, while wins at Donington Park and Le Mans in 1987 helped him finish runner-up to Stefano Modena in the championship.

James Hunt's verdict: He has shown flashes of ability in F3000. Whether the inconsistencies are his or his car's I don't know.

RENÉ ARNOUX *No. 25*

Ligier–Judd
Born 4.7.48 French
GPs contested 126
Best results
  Wins 7
  1980 BRE, SA; 1982 FRA, ITA; 1983 CAN, GER, HOL
  2nd 9; *3rd* 6; *4th* 7; *5th* 7; *6th* 5
WC placings
  1979 8th (17 points); 1980 6th (29); 1981 9th (11); 1982 6th (28); 1983 3rd (49); 1984 6th (29); 1985 17th (3); 1986 8th (14); 1987 19th (1)

The London-based Frenchman with a twinkle in his eye is the oldest GP driver on the circuit (he will be 40 on 4 July) and one of the most experienced, but he's never quite produced the goods.

He drove for Martini *and* Surtees in 1978 (his first F1 drive was in Belgium), Renault 1979–82, Ferrari 1983–5 and Ligier since then. If his worst spell in F1 was in 1985 when he was replaced after the very first race by Stefan Johansson, he did little better in 1987, managing just 1 point from 14 starts.

James Hunt's verdict: I gather that it is a matter of sponsorship that he continues to drive for Ligier. I can't see any other reason to have him.

STEFAN JOHANSSON   *No. 26*

Ligier–Judd
Born   8.9.56   Swedish
GPs contested   60
Best results
   2nd 4; *3rd* 7; *4th* 7; *5th* 3; *6th* 3
WC placings
   1984 16th (3 points); 1985 7th (26); 1986 5th (23); 1987 6th (30)

Virtually English – he has lived in London and rates Silverstone and

Brands Hatch as his favourite tracks – the immensely likeable 31-year-old Swede is now on a downward curve. He won the British F3 title in 1980 and was an F2 winner with Toleman in the following year. He made his F1 debut with Spirit at the British GP in 1983 (having had a brief attempt with Shadow in1979 when he twice failed to qualify). He started 1984 with Toleman before moving to Tyrrell, then joined Ferrari in 1986 and McLaren in 1987. He has had some great chances with top teams but has not capitalised on those drives.

James Hunt's verdict: I think his F1 career is probably over. He basically proved at both Ferrari (1986) and McLaren (1987) that, having had the opportunity, whilst he's a competent back-up driver, he's not quick enough. Without the ability No. 2s get their two or three seasons in F1. Once they've proved they are not going to be a top driver, they're out. Stefan's not good enough.

MICHELE ALBORETO   *No. 27*

Ferrari
Born   23.12.56   Italian
GPs contested   105
Best results
   Wins   5
   1982 VEG; 1983 USAE; 1984 BEL; 1985 CAN, GER
   2nd 8; *3rd* 6; *4th* 8; *5th* 3; *6th* 3

WC placings
   1982 7th (25 points); 1983
   12th (10); 1984 4th (30.5);
   1985 2nd (53); 1986 8th (14);
   1987 7th (17)

Spaghetti Bolognese, spy stories and tennis are what this 31-year-old likes to eat, read and play. He also has the best of both worlds by living in Milan and Monte Carlo. But perhaps his Italian temperament has got the better of him during the last two seasons, when his supposedly less-experienced team-mates – Stefan Johansson in 1986 and Gerhard Berger in 1987 – consistently outdrove him. When things are good at Ferrari they are good for Alboreto. After three years with Tyrrell learning the trade (his F1 debut was at San Marino in 1981), he moved to Maranello in 1984 and the following year could have won the Drivers' Championship but for a bad run of luck at the end of the season. After a promising start to 1987, an appalling run of retirements spelt disaster until Michele managed a 4th in Japan and 2nd in Australia, both behind Berger.

James Hunt's verdict: I would have thought that as he failed to respond to Berger's extra speed his days at Ferrari were reasonably numbered, but Michele re-signed for the team before Berger finished on top.

GERHARD BERGER   No. 28

Ferrari
Born   27.8.59   Austrian
GPs contested   52
Best results
   Wins   3
   1986 MEX; 1987 JAP, AUS
   2nd 1; *3rd* 1; *4th* 4; *5th* 2; *6th* 4
WC placings
   1984 21st (1 point); 1985 17th
   (3); 1986 7th (17); 1987 5th
   (36)

A man with a formidable national past to live up to (*see below*), the 28-year-old Innsbruck-based Austrian could be on the verge of that 'big' breakthrough. He really came good at the end of 1987

with two fine victories, although by then the WC was decided. This will be only his fifth year behind an F1 wheel – he started in 1984 with four races in the ATS (the first his home GP), moved to Arrows (1985), Benetton (1986) and Ferrari (1987), where he outdrove his number one driver and team-mate Michele Alboreto.

James Hunt's verdict: Gerhard is showing an outstanding talent, continuing a tradition that was started by Jochen Rindt and followed up by Niki Lauda, of always having a top Austrian driver around. Berger seems to be in the Rindt mould rather than the Lauda, but he's very fast and gaining experience all the time.

YANNICK DALMAS   *No. 29*

Larrousse–Lola
Born   28.7.61   French
GPs contested   3
Best results
   5th 1

A new entrant into the tough world of F1, this 27-year-old Frenchman from Toulon could be one to watch. He acquitted himself well in Formula Renault, F3 and F3000 before joining Philippe Alliot in 1987 for Lola's first two-car race, in Mexico. He actually finished 5th in Australia, in only his third F1 outing, but the points did not count as he was

driving a second team car which had only just been registered.

James Hunt's verdict: Dalmas is a driver in the Prost mould, in that he's very much a thinking driver. He's a good charger in a race. I've seen more of him in F3000 than in F1 and, although he didn't have a good season in F3000, that was a lot to do with his car. When the machinery was right he was outstandingly good. He confirmed his promise in the few races he has driven so far in F1.

PHILIPPE ALLIOT   *No. 30*

Larrousse–Lola
Born   27.7.54   French
GPs contested   48
Best results
   6th 4
WC placings
   1986 18th (1 point); 1987 16th (3)

Past record suggests the 33-year-old Frenchman as one of the current crop of drivers most unlikely to succeed. But to be fair he drove for his first four seasons in uncompetitive machinery – RAM in 1984–5, Ligier in 1986 and Lola in 1987. His previous career included third place in the 1981 European F3 championship and third in the 1983 Le Mans 24-hour race.

James Hunt's verdict: He'll never make a GP driver until he learns to keep his car on the road. He's had long enough, and leopards tend not to change their spots.

Osella. He retired on lap 27. A former F3000 driver, he was also 125cc kart world champion in 1984.

James Hunt's verdict: I don't know much about him. He didn't do anything special in F3000.

OSCAR LARRAURI   No. 32

EuroBrun–Cosworth
Born   19.8.54   Argentinian
GPs contested   0

'Poppy', as the popular Larrauri is

GABRIELE TARQUINI   No. 31

Coloni–Cosworth
Born   2.3.62   Italian
GPs contested   1

Another Italian to try his hand at F1, the 26-year-old managed to squeeze into last position on the grid in his only race – at Imola for the 1987 San Marino GP with

known, began F3 racing in Europe in 1981 and became European champion with 7 wins in 1982. Since then his major achievements have been in sports-car racing: driving for Brun Motorsport he won at Jerez in 1986 and helped the team to the Group C World Championship for that season.

James Hunt's verdict: Too early to assess his chances.

STEFANO MODENA   *No. 33*

EuroBrun–Cosworth
Born   12.5.63   Italian
GPs contested   1

Stefano made his F1 debut at the end of 1987 with Brabham at Adelaide. He qualified in 15th but was forced to retire on lap 32 with heat exhaustion. From Modena, he began racing karts in 1975, becoming world junior champion. In 1987 he had a

superb F3000 season, taking the European championship.

James Hunt's verdict: Stefano has outstanding talent. He will be the next Italian driving for Ferrari – possibly next season.

ALEX CAFFI   *No. 36*

Dallara–Cosworth
Born   18.3.64   Italian
GPs contested   15

Another Italian in the F1 world, Alex has achieved nothing in 15 outings over two years with Osella. The 24-year-old lives in Bergamo, and came to F1 via F3.

James Hunt's verdict: Not up to GP standard. Not competent, but there again he was not in a very good car.

DRIVERS' WORLD CHAMPIONSHIP

1950   Giuseppe Farina, ITA (Alfa-Romeo)
1951   Juan-Manuel Fangio, ARG (Alfa-Romeo)
1952   Alberto Ascari, ITA (Ferrari)
1953   Ascari (Ferrari)
1954   Fangio (Maserati/Mercedes)
1955   Fangio (Mercedes)
1956   Fangio (Lancia/Ferrari)
1957   Fangio (Maserati)
1958   Mike Hawthorn, GB (Ferrari)
1959   Jack Brabham, AUS (Cooper Climax)
1960   Brabham (Cooper Climax)
1961   Phil HIll, USA (Ferrari)
1962   Graham Hill, GB (BRM)
1963   Jim Clark, GB (Lotus Climax)
1964   John Surtees, GB (Ferrari)
1965   Clark (Lotus Climax)
1966   Brabham (Brabham Repco)
1967   Denis Hulme, NZ (Brabham Repco)
1968   G. Hill (Lotus Ford)
1969   Jackie Stewart, GB (Matra Ford)
1970   Jochen Rindt, AUT (Lotus Ford)
1971   Stewart (Tyrrell Ford)
1972   Emerson Fittipaldi, BRE (Lotus Ford)
1973   Stewart (Tyrrell Ford)
1974   Fittipaldi (McLaren Ford)
1975   Niki Lauda, AUT (Ferrari)
1976   James Hunt, GB (McLaren Ford)
1977   Lauda (Ferrari)
1978   Mario Andretti, USA (Lotus Ford)
1979   Jody Scheckter, SA (Ferrari)
1980   Alan Jones, AUS (Williams Ford)
1981   Nelson Piquet, BRE (Brabham Ford)
1982   Keke Rosberg, FIN (Williams Ford)
1983   Piquet (Brabham BMW Turbo)
1984   Lauda (McLaren TAG/Porsche Turbo)
1985   Alain Prost, FRA (McLaren TAG/Porsche Turbo)
1986   Prost (McLaren TAG/Porsche Turbo)
1987   Piquet (Williams Honda Turbo)

GP Wins		*Races Contested*
28	Alain Prost	121
27	Jackie Stewart	99
25	Jim Clark	72
25	Niki Lauda	171
24	Juan-Manuel Fangio	51
20	Nelson Piquet	141
16	Stirling Moss	66
14	Jack Brabham	126
14	Emerson Fittipaldi	144
14	Graham Hill	176
13	Alberto Ascari	32
13	Nigel Mansell	104
12	Alan Jones	116
12	Mario Andretti	128
12	Carlos Reutemann	146
10	James Hunt	92
10	Jody Scheckter	112
10	Ronnie Peterson	123

Other current drivers		
7	René Arnoux	126
6	Ayrton Senna	62
5	Michele Alboreto	105
3	Gerhard Berger	52
2	Riccardo Patrese	160

Pole Positions

33 Jim Clark
28 Juan-Manuel Fangio
24 Niki Lauda
24 Nelson Piquet
18 Mario Andretti
18 René Arnoux
17 Jackie Stewart
16 Stirling Moss
16 Alain Prost
16 Ayrton Senna
14 Alberto Ascari
14 James Hunt
14 Ronnie Peterson
13 Jack Brabham
13 Graham Hill
13 Jacky Ickx
12 Nigel Mansell
10 Jochen Rindt

Fastest Laps

27 Jim Clark
25 Niki Lauda
23 Juan-Manuel Fangio
23 Nelson Piquet
20 Stirling Moss
20 Alain Prost
15 Clay Regazzoni
15 Jackie Stewart
14 Jacky Ickx
13 Alan Jones
12 René Arnoux
11 Alberto Ascari
11 John Surtees
10 Mario Andretti
10 Jack Brabham
10 Graham Hill

Others

3 Gerhard Berger
2 Michele Alboreto
2 Riccardo Patrese
1 Andrea De Cesaris

Others

9 Nigel Mansell
7 Ayrton Senna
5 Gerhard Berger
3 Michele Alboreto
3 Riccardo Patrese
2 Derek Warwick
1 Andrea De Cesaris

Since 1961 9 points have been awarded for first place, 6 for 2nd, 4 for 3rd, 3 for 4th, 2 for 5th and 1 for 6th. Drivers count only their best 11 results out of 16 GPs.

CONSTRUCTORS' WORLD CHAMPIONSHIP
Called 'Formula One Constructors'
Championship' until 1982

1958	Vanwall	1968	Lotus	1978	Lotus
1959	Cooper	1969	Matra	1979	Ferrari
1960	Cooper	1970	Lotus	1980	Williams
1961	Ferrari	1971	Tyrrell	1981	Williams
1962	BRM	1972	Lotus	1982	Ferrari
1963	Lotus	1973	Lotus	1983	Ferrari
1964	Ferrari	1974	McLaren	1984	McLaren
1965	Lotus	1975	Ferrari	1985	McLaren
1966	Brabham	1976	Ferrari	1986	Williams
1967	Brabham	1977	Ferrari	1987	Williams

1988 WORLD CHAMPIONSHIP

April 3	Brazil	July 24	Germany
May 1	San Marino	August 7	Hungary
May 15	Monaco	August 28	Belgium
May 29	Mexico	September 11	Italy
June 12	Canada	September 25	Portugal
June 19	United States	October 2	Spain
July 3	France	October 30	Japan
July 10	Great Britain	November 13	Australia

ABBREVIATIONS

ARG	Argentina	F1	Formula One	JAP	Japan
AUS	Australia	F2	Formula Two	MEX	Mexico
AUT	Austria	F3	Formula Three	MON	Monaco
BEL	Belgium	F3000	Formula 3000	POR	Portugal
BRE	Brazil	GB	Great Britain	RSM	San Marino
CAN	Canada	GER	Germany	SA	South Africa
ESP	Spain	GP	Grand Prix	USAE	Eastern United States
EUR	Europe	HOL	Holland	USAW	Western United States
FF	Formula Ford	HON	Hungary	VEG	Las Vegas
FRA	France	ITA	Italy	WC	World Championship

Opposite *The driver with the most vital statistic of all: Alain Prost, now with a record 29 GP wins after his victory in Brazil in 1988*

British Grand Prix Results 1950–1959

	1950	1951	1952	1953	1954	1955	1956	1957	1958	1959
Date	13 May	14 July	19 July	18 July	17 July	16 July	14 July	20 July	19 July	18 July
Track	Silverstone	Silverstone	Silverstone	Silverstone	Silverstone	Aintree	Silverstone	Aintree	Silverstone	Aintree
Laps	70	90	85	90	90	90	101	90	75	75
Distance	202.23 miles	260 miles	248.7 miles	263.3 miles	263.3 miles	270 miles	295.5 miles	270 miles	219.5 miles	225 miles
Pole	G.Farina	F.Gonzalez	G.Farina	A.Ascari	J.M.Fangio	S.Moss	S.Moss	S.Moss	S.Moss	J.Brabham
	1m.50.8s.	1m.44.4s.	1m.50.0s.	1m.48.0s.	1m.50.0s.	2m.00.4s.	1m.41.0s.	2m.00.2s.	1m.39.4s.	1m.58.0s.
1st	G.Farina	F.Gonzalez	A.Ascari	A.Ascari	F.Gonzalez	S.Moss	J.M.Fangio	S.Moss/T.Brooks	P.Collins	J.Brabham
	Alfa-Romeo	Ferrari	Ferrari	Ferrari	Ferrari	Mercedes	Ferrari	Vanwall	Ferrari	Cooper Climax
	2hrs.13m.23.6s.	2hrs.42m.18.2s.	2hrs.44m.11s.	2hrs.50m.	2hrs.56m.14s.	3hrs.7m.21.2s.	2hrs.59m.47.0s.	3hrs.6m.37.8s.	2hrs.9m.4.2s.	2hrs.30m.11.6s.
	90.95 mph	96.11 mph	90.92 mph	92.97 mph	89.69 mph	86.47 mph	98.65 mph	86.8 mph	102.05 mph	89.88 mph
2nd	L.Fagioli	J.M.Fangio	P.Taruffi	J.M.Fangio	M.Hawthorn	J.M.Fangio	A.DePortago/ P.Collins	L.Musso	M.Hawthorn	S.Moss
3rd	R.Parnell	L.Villoresi	M.Hawthorn	G.Farina	O.Marimon	K.Kling	J.Behra	M.Hawthorn	R.Salvadori	B.McLaren
4th	Y.Giraud-Cabantous	F.Bonetto	D.Poore	F.Gonzalez	J.M.Fangio	P.Taruffi	J.Fairman	M.Trintignant	S.Lewis-Evans	H.Schell
5th	L.Rosier	R.Parnell	E.Thompson	M.Hawthorn	M.Trintignant	L.Musso	H.Gould	R.Salvadori	H.Schell	M.Trintignant
6th	F.R.Gerard	C.Sanesi	G.Farina	F.Bonetto	R.Mieres	M.Hawthorn/ E.Castellotti	L.Villoresi	F.R.Gerard	J.Brabham	R.Salvadori
Fastest	G.Farina	G.Farina	A.Ascari	A.Ascari	7 drivers*	S.Moss	S.Moss	S.Moss	M.Hawthorn	Moss/McLaren
lap	1m.50.6s.	1m.44.0s.	1m.52.0s.	1m.50.0s.	1m.50.0s.	2m.00.4s.	1m.43.2s.	1m.59.2s.	1m.40.8s.	1m.57.0s.
	94.55 mph	99.99 mph	94.08 mph	95.79 mph	95.79 mph	89.7 mph	102.104 mph	90.6 mph	104.5 mph	92.31 mph

*Fangio, Ascari, Hawthorn, Moss, Marimon, Behra, Gonzalez.

British Grand Prix Results 1960-1969

	1960	1961	1962	1963	1964	1965	1966	1967	1968	1969
Date	16 July	15 July	21 July	20 July	11 July	10 July	16 July	15 July	20 July	19 July
Track	Silverstone	Aintree	Aintree	Silverstone	Brands Hatch	Silverstone	Brands Hatch	Silverstone	Brands Hatch	Silverstone
Laps	77	75	75	82	80	80	80	80	80	84
Distance	225.3 miles	225 miles	225 miles	240 miles	212 miles	234 miles	212 miles	234 miles	212 miles	245.87 miles
Pole	J.Brabham	P.Hill	J.Clark	J.Clark	J.Clark	J.Clark	J.Brabham	J.Clark	G.Hill	J.Rindt
	1m.34.6s.	1m.58.8s.	1m.53.6s.	1m.34.4s.	1m.38.1s.	1m.30.8s.	1m.34.5s.	1m.25.3s.	1m.28.9s.	1m.20.8s.
1st	J.Brabham	W.von Trips	J.Clark	J.Clark	J.Clark	J.Clark	J.Brabham	J.Clark	J.Siffert	J.Stewart
	Cooper Climax	Ferrari	Lotus Climax	Lotus Climax	Lotus Climax	Lotus Climax	Brabham Repco	Lotus Ford	Lotus Ford	Matra Ford
	2hrs.4m.24.6s.	2hrs.40m.53.6s.	2hrs.26m.20.8s.	2hrs.14m.9.6s.	2hrs.15m.7.0s.	2hrs.5m.25.4s.	2hrs.13m.13.4s.	1hr.59m.25.6s.	2hrs.1m.20.3s.	1hr.55m.55.6s.
	108.69 mph	83.91 mph	92.25 mph	107.75 mph	94.14 mph	112.02 mph	95.48 mph	117.64 mph	104.83 mph	127.25 mph
2nd	J.Surtees	P.Hill	J.Surtees	J.Surtees	G.Hill	G.Hill	D.Hulme	D.Hulme	C.Amon	J.Ickx
3rd	I.Ireland	R.Ginther	B.McLaren	G.Hill	J.Surtees	J.Surtees	G.Hill	C.Amon	J.Ickx	B.McLaren
4th	B.McLaren	J.Brabham	G.Hill	R.Ginther	J.Brabham	M.Spence	J.Clark	J.Brabham	D.Hulme	J.Rindt
5th	T.Brooks	J.Bonnier	J.Brabham	L.Bandini	L.Bandini	J.Stewart	J.Rindt	P.Rodriguez	J.Surtees	P.Courage
6th	W.von Trips	R.Salvadori	T.Maggs	J.Hall	P.Hill	D.Gurney	B.McLaren	J.Surtees	J.Stewart	V.Elford
Fastest	G.Hill	T.Brooks	J.Clark	J.Surtees	J.Clark	G.Hill	J.Brabham	D.Hulme	J.Siffert	J.Stewart
lap	1m.34.4s.	1m.57.8s.	1m.55.0s.	1m.36.0s.	1m.38.8s.	1m.32.2s.	1m.37.0s.	1m.27.0s.	1m.29.7s.	1m.21.3s.
	111.62 mph	91.68 mph	93.91 mph	109.76 mph	96.56 mph	114.29 mph	98.35 mph	121.12 mph	106.35 mph	129.61 mph

British Grand Prix Results 1970–1979

	1970	1971	1972	1973	1974	1975	1976	1977	1978	1979
Date	18 July	17 July	15 July	14 July	20 July	19 July	18 July	16 July	16 July	14 July
Track	Brands Hatch	Silverstone	Brands Hatch	Silverstone	Brands Hatch	Silverstone	Brands Hatch	Silverstone	Brands Hatch	Silverstone
Laps	80	68	76	67	75	67	76*	68	76	68
Distance	212 miles	199 miles	201.4 miles	196.1 miles	198.75 miles	196.44 miles	198.63 miles*	200.56 miles	198.63 miles	200.56 miles
Pole	J.Rindt	C.Regazzoni	E.Fittipaldi	R.Peterson	N.Lauda	T.Pryce	N.Lauda	J.Hunt	R.Peterson	A.Jones
	1m.24.8s.	1m.18.1s.	1m.22.2s.	1m.16.3s.	1m.19.7s.	1m.19.36s.	1m.19.35s.	1m.18.49s.	1m.16.8s.	1m.11.88s.
1st	J.Rindt	J.Stewart	E.Fittipaldi	P.Revson	J.Scheckter	E.Fittipaldi	N.Lauda	J.Hunt	C.Reutemann	C.Regazzoni
	Lotus Ford	Tyrrell Ford	Lotus Ford	McLaren Ford	Tyrrell Ford	McLaren Ford	Ferrari	McLaren Ford	Ferrari	Williams Ford
	1hr.57m.2.0s.	1hr.31m.31.5s.	1hr.47m.50.2s.	1hr.29m.18.5s.	1hr.43m.02.2s.	1hr.22m.05.0s.	1hr.44m.19.66s.	1hr.31m.46.06s.	1hr.42m.12.39s.	1hr.26m.11.17s.
	108.69 mph	130.48 mph	112.06 mph	131.75 mph	115.73 mph	120.04 mph	115.04 mph	130.36 mph	116.61 mph	138.80 mph
2nd	J.Brabham	R.Peterson	J.Stewart	R.Peterson	E.Fittipaldi	C.Pace	J.Scheckter	N.Lauda	N.Lauda	R.Arnoux
3rd	D.Hulme	E.Fittipaldi	P.Revson	D.Hulme	J.Ickx	J.Scheckter	J.Watson	G.Nilsson	J.Watson	J.-P.Jarier
4th	C.Regazzoni	H.Pescarolo	C.Amon	J.Hunt	C.Regazzoni	J.Hunt	T.Pryce	J.Mass	P.Depailler	J.Watson
5th	C.Amon	R.Stommelen	D.Hulme	F.Cevert	N.Lauda	M.Donohue	A.Jones	H.Stuck	H.Stuck	J.Scheckter
6th	G.Hill	J.Surtees	A.Merzario	C.Reutemann	C.Reutemann	V.Brambilla	E.Fittipaldi	J.Laffite	P.Tambay	J.Ickx
Fastest	J.Brabham	J.Stewart	J.Stewart	J.Hunt	N.Lauda	C.Regazzoni	N.Lauda	J.Hunt	N.Lauda	C.Regazzoni
lap	1m.25.9s.	1m.19.9s.	1m.24.0s.	1m.18.6s.	1m.21.1s.	1m.20.9s.	1m.19.91s.	1m.19.60s.	1m.18.60s.	1m.14.40s.
	111.06 mph	131.88 mph	113.57 mph	134.06 mph	117.63 mph	130.47 mph	117.74 mph	133.375 mph	120.41 mph	142.7 mph

* Because of rain reduced to 56 laps, 165.17 miles.

British Grand Prix Results 1980–1987

	1980	1981	1982	1983	1984	1985	1986	1987
Date	13 July	18 July	18 July	16 July	22 July	21 July	13 July	12 July
Track	Brands Hatch	Silverstone	Brands Hatch	Silverstone	Brands Hatch	Silverstone	Brands Hatch	Silverstone
Laps	76	68	76	67	71	65	75	65
Distance	199.83 miles	200.558 miles	199.83 miles	197.608 miles	186.685 miles	191.709 miles	197.203 miles	192.985 miles
Pole	D.Pironi	R.Arnoux	K.Rosberg	R.Arnoux	N.Piquet	K.Rosberg	N.Piquet	N.Piquet
	1m.11.007s.	1m.11.00s.	1m.09.54s.	1m.09.462s.	1m.10.869s.	1m.05.591s.	1m.06.961s.	1m.07.110s.
1st	A.Jones	J.Watson	N.Lauda	A.Prost	N.Lauda	A.Prost	N.Mansell	N.Mansell
	Williams Ford	McLaren Ford	McLaren Ford	Renault Turbo	McLaren TAG	McLaren TAG	Williams Honda	Williams Honda
					Porsche	Porsche	Turbo	Turbo
	1hr.34m.49.228s.	1hr.26m.54.8s.	1hr.35m.33.812s.	1hr.24m.39.78s.	1hr.29m.28.532s.	1hr.18m.10.436s.	1hr.30m.38.471s.	1hr.19m.11.780s.
	126.424 mph	138.45 mph	125.465 mph	140.043 mph	125.186 mph	147.109 mph	130.505 mph	146.208 mph
2nd	N.Piquet	C.Reutemann	D.Pironi	N.Piquet	D.Warwick	M.Alboreto	N.Piquet	N.Piquet
3rd	C.Reutemann	J.Laffite	P.Tambay	P.Tambay	A.Senna	J.Laffite	A.Prost	A.Senna
4th	D.Daly	E.Cheever	E.De Angelis	N.Mansell	E.De Angelis	N.Piquet	R.Arnoux	S.Nakajima
5th	J.-P.Jarier	H.Rebaque	D.Daly	R.Arnoux	M.Alboreto	D.Warwick	M.Brundle	D.Warwick
6th	A.Prost	S.Borgudd	A.Prost	N.Lauda	R.Arnoux	M.Surer	P.Streiff	T.Fabi
Fastest lap	D.Pironi	R.Arnoux	B.Henton	A.Prost	N.Lauda	A.Prost	N.Mansell	N.Mansell
	1m.12.368s.	1m.15.067s.	1m.13.028s.	1m.14.212s.	1m.13.191s.	1m.09.886s.	1m.09.593s.	1m.09.832s.
	130.8 mph	141.443 mph	129.618 mph	143.073 mph	129.329 mph	151.897 mph	135.980 mph	153.059 mph

THE BRABHAM RECORD 1972-87

1972　Drivers – Graham Hill, Carlos Reutemann
　　　Wins – 0 (although Reutemann won the non-championship Brazilian Grand Prix)

1973　Drivers – Reutemann, Wilson Fittipaldi, John Watson, Rolf Stommelen
　　　Wins – 0

1974　Drivers – Reutemann, R. Von Open, Carlos Pace, Watson
　　　Wins – 3 (Reutemann – South Africa, Austria, Watkins Glen)

1975　Drivers – Reutemann, Pace
　　　Wins – 2 (Pace – Brazil; Reutemann – Germany)

1976　Drivers – Reutemann, Pace
　　　Wins – 0

1977　Drivers – Watson, Pace, Hans Stuck
　　　Wins – 0

1978　Drivers – Niki Lauda, Watson
　　　Wins – 2 (Lauda – Sweden, Italy)

1979　Drivers – Lauda, Nelson Piquet
　　　Wins – 0 (although Lauda won the non-championship Gran Premio Dino Ferrari at Imola)

1980　Drivers – Piquet, R. Zunino, Hector Rebaque
　　　Wins – 3 (Piquet – Long Beach, Holland, Italy)

1981　Drivers – Piquet, Rebaque
　　　Wins – 3 (Piquet – Argentina, San Marino, Germany)
　　　Piquet World Champion

1982　Drivers – Piquet, Riccardo Patrese
　　　Wins – 2 (Patrese – Monaco; Piquet – Canada)

1983　Drivers – Piquet, Patrese
　　　Wins – 4 (Piquet – Brazil, Italy, Europe; Patrese – South Africa)
　　　Piquet World Champion

1984　Drivers – Piquet, Teo Fabi, Corrado Fabi
　　　Wins – 2 (Piquet – Canada, Detroit)

1985　Drivers – Piquet, Marc Surer, François Hesnault
　　　Wins – 1 (Piquet – France)

1986　Drivers – Patrese, Elio De Angelis, Derek Warwick
　　　Wins – 0

1987　Drivers – Patrese, Andrea De Cesaris
　　　Wins – 0

Opposite *Ayrton Senna on home ground, Brazil 1987*

GP - THE TELEVISION FACTS

	1986	1987	% change
No. of countries	47	52	+10.6
Total broadcasts	580	681	+17.4
Total minutes	59,180	68,987	+16.6
Total minutes live	41,091	46,578	+13.4
Total minutes deferred	18,089	22,409	+24.0
Total countries taking news coverage	84	86	+2.4
Total minutes of all coverage	74,852	85,572	+14.3
Total viewers of live or deferred broadcasts	1,435,222,000	1,449,316,000	+0.98
Average per GP	89,701,375	90,582,250	+0.98

© FOCA

PICTURE CREDITS

Most of the pictures in this book were supplied by Steven Tee and L.A.T. Photographic. Acknowledgement is also due to the following picture sources:

Pages 58 top, 59 bottom, Allsport; 67, BBC; 8 bottom, 94, 118, 121, 124 bottom, 124 inset, 125, 126 right, 128, 134, BBC Hulton Picture Library; 175, J Cochin/Explorer; 22 bottom right, Arthur Griffin; 8 top, 15, Alain Guillou; 116, 124 top, 131, The Keystone Collection; 133, The Kobal Collection; 63 inset, MAO; 145 top, 152, 153 bottom, 158 top, 159 left, Rex Features Limited; 28 top, 145 bottom, 148 right, 149 right, Frank Spooner Pictures/Gamma; 97 inset, Keith Sutton; 16, 77, 86 bottom, 97, 111, 143 top; Stuart Sykes; front and back cover, Colin Taylor Productions; 25, 29, 31, 32 bottom, 66 top, 68 top, 71 left, 89 top, 91 right, 111 centre, 138, 139, 148 left, 151, 154, 155 top, 157, 161 right, 162 bottom left, John Townsend; 160 right, US Press.

Opposite *Warning note: Gerhard Berger (left) and Michele Alboreto on their way to a Ferrari one-two at Adelaide, 1987*

Page 176 *Heart of the matter*